A Rum Do!

Smuggling in and around Robin Hood's Bay

Patricia Labistour

MARINE ARTS PUBLICATIONS

A Rum Do!
Smuggling
in and around
Robin Hood's Bay

Cliffs at Peak - (Ravenscar)
steel engraving dated 1836

First published 1996 by Marine Arts Publications,
"Seascape",
Robin Hood's Bay,
Whitby, North Yorkshire,
England. YO22 4SH.

ISBN 0-9516184-1-5
A Rum Do!

Design and page planning by
Graham Boddy

Front cover painting by
Edward H. Simpson

Line drawings © by
John Gilman

Photography © by
Graham Boddy
Roma Hodgson
Rosemary Bowman
Patricia Labistour

Reproduction by Image Colourprint Ltd,
Grange Park Lane,
Willerby, East Yorkshire
HU10 6EB

For Léon.........
my guiding light.

Contents

Line drawings by John Gilman

Photo credits:-
Graham Boddy:- Nos 1, 2, 3, 4, 7, 8, 9, 10,
                14, 15, 16, 17, 18, 19, 20, 22.
                a, b, d, e, g, h, i, j.
Roma Hodgson:- Nos 21.
                k, p, q, r.
Rosemary Bowman:- m, n.
Pat Labistour:- Nos 5, 6, 11, 12, 13.
                f, l, o.

Acknowledgements

Throughout the preparation of this book, I have been fortunate in having the support of a number of good friends.

First and foremost I treasure the full and critical appraisal of my late husband, Léon, who initially encouraged its production and saw the text well into its final stages. Sadly, he was not to see it in print.

My associations with photographer Graham Boddy, and illustrator John Gilman, go back in both instances to chance meetings in 'Bay in the late '60's, from which developed long standing mutual friendships. Graham's artistic photographer's eye, capturing so many of the varied moods of 'Bay in all seasons, has produced some memorable pictures to complement the text. He has also nursed the whole production through the printing process to its final binding and completion. My thanks also to his wife, Pat, for her patient proof reading, and to Roma Hodgson for some lovely 'winter' photography.

John Gilman is a retired headmaster, with a fine hand for line drawings and a love of all things nautical. His skilful and evocative art work has recreated the atmosphere of the past, and greatly enhanced the pages. John's other interests include miniature ship modelling and writing, and he has published a number of books, ranging from history of his native Exmoor to film making.

For many years we have enjoyed owning a water colour by the late Edward H. Simpson, showing our home on the cliff, and I am grateful to his nephew, Clive Potts, for giving permission for this to be reproduced as the cover for this book.

My good friend Rosemary Bowman was 'on the spot' with her camera soon after one of the accidental 'demolition' jobs on The Old Forge. I am happy that she has agreed to two of her photographs being used to illustrate the point that 'Bay Bank can be a steep and dangerous approach to the village!

I acknowledge information obtained from publications by John Leland, Thomas Hinderwell, W.Theakston, Mathew Galtrey, E.Finden, John Wesley, Admiral Vernon, Young and Charlton, E.Keble Chatterton, Shaw Jeffrey, Hugh P.Kendall, Jack Dykes, John Tindale, G.Bernard Wood, J.R.Harrison, HM Customs and Excise, Whitby Gazette, Yorkshire Evening Post, and Newcastle Chronicle. Also from conversations with 'old locals' especially the late John S.Jackson, Sampson Thompson and Stanley Cooper.

I am also indebted to the literary agents A.P.Watt Ltd on behalf of The National Trust for Places of Historic Interest or Natural Beauty, to include Rudyard Kipling's 'The Smuggler's Song' from 'Puck of Pook's Hill'.

Finally, thanks to all the staff at Image Colourprint Ltd, for their interest and advice throughout.

i

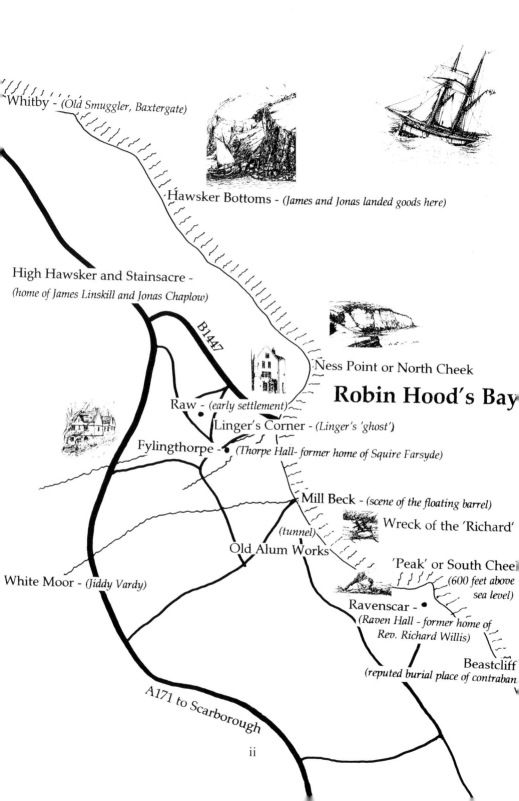

Whitby - *(Old Smuggler, Baxtergate)*

Hawsker Bottoms - *(James and Jonas landed goods here)*

High Hawsker and Stainsacre -
(home of James Linskill and Jonas Chaplow)

B1447

Ness Point or North Cheek

Robin Hood's Bay

Raw - *(early settlement)*

Linger's Corner - *(Linger's 'ghost')*

Fylingthorpe - *(Thorpe Hall- former home of Squire Farsyde)*

Mill Beck - *(scene of the floating barrel)*

(tunnel)

Wreck of the 'Richard'

Old Alum Works

'Peak' or South Cheek
*(600 feet above
sea level)*

White Moor - *(Jiddy Vardy)*

Ravenscar -
*(Raven Hall - former home of
Rev. Richard Willis)*

Beastcliff
(reputed burial place of contraban

A171 to Scarborough

Thorpe Hall, the former home of
Squire Farsyde, one of the members
of a highly successful smuggling syndicate.
A stone slab set into his lawn concealed a
handy underground storage chamber for contraband.

Foreword

I have known and loved Robin Hood's Bay from the time I took my first stumbling steps on its beach at a very tender age, never imagining in the dream-like holidays of childhood which followed, each glorious long summer, that it would eventually become my permanent home, and the place where I would teach my own daughter to walk on that very same stretch of sun-warmed sand.

So it was that the kind hand of fate led us to follow up a newspaper advertisement whilst searching for a new home 'somewhere by the sea' immediately prior to marriage in 1967. The three hundred year old 'house on the cliff' (shown on the cover) charmed us, in spite of its - then - somewhat precarious position. Since 1976, however, it has, with the rest of the cliff clinging cottages, enjoyed the protection of one of the largest sea walls in Britain.

The joys of newly wedded life, combined with the advantage of being able to fish actually out of the kitchen window, and the excitement of high tides and strong winds hurling sea spray high over the top of the house, confirmed that, in spite of family opinion that we were crazy, this was 'the place for us'. Seeing the house for the first time, my mother prudently bought us a lifebelt for a wedding present; it has remained our house sign to this day!

Now, thirty years on, and steeped in its charismatic atmosphere and history, my love for 'Bay in its setting of unsurpassable beauty, is deeper than ever; from each morning when the sun rises from the sea in a riot of brilliant colour, through to the nights of dappled moonshine on the water, it weaves its magical spell of things past, present, and yet to come.

Pat Labistour,
"Seascape",
Robin Hood's Bay.
1996

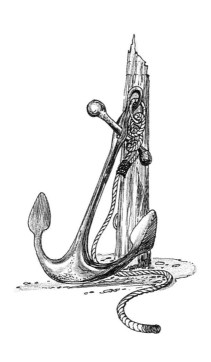

Introduction

The romantic name of Robin Hood's Bay draws visitors from world wide, to delight in its unique beauty, explore its quaint streets, and lose themselves in its timeless past.

The stories in this book will 'spirit' you back in time to the Robin Hood's Bay of the eighteenth century, when the village was one of the most important for smuggling on the whole of the Yorkshire coast.

Follow in the shadowy footsteps of sea farers long since gone, but before you read on, take warning from Rudyard Kipling's poem for you are treading dangerous ground........

If you wake at midnight, and hear a horse's feet,
  Don't go drawing back the blind, or looking in the street.
Them that asks no questions isn't told a lie,
  Watch the wall, my darling, while the Gentlemen go by!

          Five and twenty ponies
          Trotting through the dark -
          Brandy for the Parson,
          'Baccy for the Clerk;
          Laces for a lady; letters for a spy;
And watch the wall, my darling, while the Gentlemen go by!

Running round the woodlump, if you chance to find
  Little barrels, roped and tarred, all full of brandy-wine,
Don't you shout to come and look, nor take 'em for your play;
  Put the brushwood back again - and they'll be gone next day!

If you see the stable-yard setting open wide;
  If you see a tired horse lying down inside;
If your mother mends a coat cut about and tore;
  If the lining's wet and warm - don't you ask no more!

If you meet King George's men, dressed in blue and red,
  You be careful what you say, and mindful what is said;
If they call you 'pretty maid' and chuck you 'neath the chin,
  Don't you tell where no one is, nor yet where no one's been!

Knocks and footsteps round the house - whistles after dark -
  You've no call for running out till the house-dogs bark.
 Trusty's here, and Pincher's here, and see how dumb they lie!
  They don't fret to follow when the Gentlemen go by!

If you do as you've been told, likely there's a chance
  You'll be give a dainty doll, all the way from France,
With a cap of Valenciennes, and a velvet hood -
  A present from the Gentlemen, along o' being good!

          Five and twenty ponies,
          Trotting through the dark -
          Brandy for the Parson,
          'Baccy for the Clerk.
Them that asks no questions isn't told a lie -
Watch the wall, my darling, while the Gentlemen go by!

                                                    Rudyard Kipling

vii

'The town is very remarkably situated;
it stands close to the sea and is in great
part built upon craggy and steep rocks,
some of which rise perpendicular from the water'

John Wesley - on his first visit to Robin Hood's Bay, Tuesday, 8 May, 1753.

Lithograph by Francis Nicholson - 1821

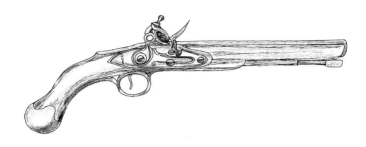

Rudyard Kipling's poem, evoking memories of the classroom, captures perfectly the excitement of the romantic picture of smuggling with its suggestion of hidden contraband, secrecy and suspicion, and a certain inbuilt fear of knowing more than was good for you regarding the activities of the 'Gentlemen'. The reality was, in fact, far from the writer's idealistic image, and anything but romantic.

Smuggling was at all times fraught with danger; it was undeniably dishonest, and the considerable risks and unpleasant penalties weighed against the advantages of making large profits from an illegal source.

Smugglers have been regarded variously as thieves and rogues: thieves because they robbed the Government - and thus their fellow men - of taxes approved by Act of Parliament; and rogues because their law breaking in carrying out their activities took them to the point of defiance. They were, however, 'acceptable' to a large section of the populace of this country, as they defied what many regarded as unjust taxation, and - more to the point - supplied many of the little luxuries of life at reasonably cheap rates!

Serious smuggling was, perhaps because of this, a recognised national 'industry' throughout a large part of the eighteenth century - in fact, becoming an enterprise that involved half the nation - and the remote Yorkshire coast villages were at its very heart.

Robin Hood's Bay was credited with being the headquarters of one of the most powerful gangs of smugglers on the north east coast, and when the trade was at its height, 'Bay was said to be the wealthiest place in England for its size!

This may be an extreme claim, but certainly, here in Robin Hood's Bay, the inhabitants of both the village and its hinterland were ideally positioned for their involvement: a secluded bay on a lonely and rugged coastline, an isolated, close-knit and suspicious village community of seafaring folk, familiar with all the moods of the wayward sea, backed by a wild and hostile hinterland of moor and bog, with minimal communication routes to the outside world, many of which were only known intimately by 'locals'. With close-packed cottages crammed into secretive huddles in narrow alleyways it made the ideal setting for such exploits. Robin Hood's Bay has, for generations, called forth comment on its remote and unique appearance.

Theakston's 'Guide to Scarborough', published in 1847, describes the village in most charming and picturesque terms: 'No place of human abode can be conceived more wild in its appearance than this village, where the tidy little edifices of the fishermen are perched, like the nests of seagulls, among the cliffs. The communication from one street to another, in some places, is so entirely cut off, that access is obtained by a plank bridge thrown over a gully. Every individual dwelling is characteristic of the neatness of a seafaring proprietor - him whom early habit has taught the true principles of the economy of space and to whom the contrast of rough and perilous hours abroad the more endears the delights of home.'

One nineteenth century 'tourist' wrote: 'The Bay Town as it is generally called, is crammed into the most surprisingly small compass, the houses being tall or short as their position in the rocky cleft necessitated, and they are built into and on top of one another to a greater extent than anywhere along the Yorkshire coast. Although the place seems big enough when one is among the houses, immediately you climb out onto the cliffs it seems to disappear in the most miraculous fashion.'

Another, highly poetic lady, saw 'Bay as 'a green hill with clusters of brown-walled red-roofed cottages clinging to its side like a crowd of red-tufted birds'. This visitor became a little adventurous, and began to explore: 'We found our way to the inaccessible-looking houses on the rock. These are built in a succession of narrow twisting alleys paved with irregular round stones, first a few stone cottages on either side, and then a flight of shallow grass-grown steps........these steps start up unexpectedly and the houses are often set at angles, turning away from one another as though they had quarrelled....... Everywhere huge nets were stretched out to dry. Rosy-cheeked children and pigs were plentiful, playing about promiscuously.'

To modern eyes, Old 'Bay is a town-planner's nightmare, with odd-shaped cottages squeezed onto any available pieces of land. Not only was building space at a premium because of the geographical siting of the village on the steep sides of a ravine, but small gardens and yards adjoining existing properties were built on to provide a home for a newly married daughter, thus contributing to the picturesque roofscape we see today. When so many of the men folk were away at sea, the women left behind preferred the close company of their own kind - always assuming that family relationships remained friendly!

John Wesley, on his first visit to Robin Hood's Bay on Tuesday, 8 May, 1753, wrote: 'The town is very remarkably situated; it stands close to the sea and is in great part built upon craggy and steep rocks, some of which rise perpendicular from the water.' The view that first impressed John Wesley would be very similar to that shown in the illustration at the beginning of this chapter. However, in 1780, only a few months after Wesley had opened the 'new preaching house' in Low Street (now Chapel Street), a massive landslide which took with it the upper end of King Street and over two hundred houses, exposed the new building to the cliff, and altered completely the appearance of the village from the seaward side. In 1798, the historian Thomas Hinderwell described it thus: 'The village once made a grotesque appearance, the houses being strangely scattered over the face of a steep cliff and some of them hanging in an awful manner on the projecting ledges of the precipice. But this place has lately sustained a great alteration by the falling of the Cliff in consequence of which the projecting houses and the pavement of the principal street, as far as the fronts of the houses on the opposite side, are ruined and a new road has been made from the landing place through the interior part of the Town.'

Another visitor, equipped with Schofield's 'Guide to Scarborough and its Environs' in 1787* discovered that 'a person well acquainted with the road is indispensible for conducting you to this place. It is by no means a good carriageway; therefore, and from its distance, is beyond the reach of an airing on horseback for ladies and is usually visited by gentlemen only', and Finden's guide to the 'Ports and Harbours of Great Britain', published in 1836, warns: 'The approach to the village is by a steep descent, which is extremely inconvenient for carriages' - a sentiment endorsed by faint-hearted and foolish twentieth century car and caravan drivers who choose to ignore the warning signs at the top of the hill!

* The full original text of Schofield's Guide with regard to Robin Hood's Bay, is amusing to modern day readers, and well worth reading, and is therefore reprinted in the appendix at the end of the book.

So much for the geographical deterrents to the place. In the eighteenth century the inhabitants were no more friendly, and, as in other similar local places, would physically deter a stranger with an unwelcoming shower of stones and mud - or worse! Distinctly unsociable, but totally understandable, when strangers posed a real threat to the secrecy of the activities which may be going on under their very noses!

The 'Bay people of those far-off days were a hardy breed; many descended from fierce Viking ancestors, they retained an independence and fortititude much to be admired - and feared! As on many other parts of the Yorkshire coast, the invading Danes, for various reasons, decided to settle, rather than return to their native land - perhaps, having burnt their boats in rash moments of celebration, they had no alternative!

The women folk, too, were not to be argued with, as they have been recorded in history as beating off the unwelcome attentions of the Press Gang with saucepans and rolling-pins - an offence which today would bring forth charges of breach of the peace, if not assault and battery, or grievous bodily harm.

Due to the remoteness of the place, there was much intermarrying, and for generations, these daunting females married hardy local men, well used to the sea, and together bred brave sons - and daughters - with the tang of sea salt in their veins. A tough breed, well suited to their surroundings, equipped with a natural cunning, born of the sheer necessity of survival in this harsh environment, and more than a match in physical strength for the Preventive men, whose thankless task was to attempt to control their illegal activities.

The stalwart nature of these fishermen and their skill in handling boats is graphically described in a letter written at the end of the reign of Elizabeth the First:- 'Truly yt may be sayd of these poor men, that they are lavish of theyr lives, who will hazard twenty or forty myles into the seas in a small troughe so thinne that the glimse of the sunne may bee seene through yt; yet at eleven or twelve of the clocke in the morninge, when they come from the sea, they sell theire whole boaty's landing for 4s., or if they doe gette a crowne, they suppose to have chaffered fayre. Three commonly come in one boate, each of them having twoe oares, which they governe by drawing one hande over the other. The boate ytselfe is built of wainscott, for shape excels all modeles for shippinge; twoe men will easily carrye ytt on lande betweene them, yet are they so secure in them at sea, that some in a storme have lývéd aboarde three dayes. Theire greateste danger is nearest home, when the waves breake dangerouslye; but they, acquainted with these seas, espyinge a broken wave reddy to overtake them, suddenly oppose the prow or sharpe ende of theyre boate unto yt, and mountinge to the top, descende downe as yt were unto a valley, hoveringe untill they espye a whole wave come rowlinge, which they observe commonly to be an odde one; whereupon mountinge with their cobble as it were a great furious horse, they rowe with might and mayne, and together with that wave drive themselves on lande.'

The area of Robin Hood's Bay has a long history, but the village itself is not actually mentioned by name until Tudor times. The district of Fylingdales has been occupied from the earliest times by Stone, Bronze and Iron Age people, and the Romans established a signal station at Ravenscar. Domesday Book refers to the area as 'Figeling', possibly derived from the ancient Norse word 'Fygling' which means 'the act of taking sea fowl'. Or an adaptation of the Old English word for a marsh - 'fygela'.

The first fishermen lived at Fyling Row (now the hamlet of Raw) about a mile from the coast, this inland settlement being safer from sea-borne attacks by pirates. These early settlers were also part farmers, and made the journey to the sea coast with their donkeys along a track which still bears the name 'Donkey Road'.

Henry VIII himself owned property in Robin Hood's Bay - King Street is named after him - and he decreed that it was 'very necessary that all the woods within the parish of Whitby, or elsewhere thereunto, shall be reserved for the maintenance of the King's cottages in Whitby and at Robin Hood's Baye'. His daughter, Queen Elizabeth the first, disposed of her 'fifty tenaments' in Robin Hood's Bay in 1536, the same year in which the topographer, Leland, in his 'Itinerary' described it as 'a fischer tounlet of twenty bootes', and in the late 1700s and early 1800s fishing was still a very viable occupation. In 1816 official fishery records state that there were five five-man boats, and thirty-five cobles. The five-man boats were 46 feet long, 16' 8" broad, 6' 3" deep, clinker-built, sharp bottomed vessels of some 58 tons. They had three masts, carried four sails, and were generally swift sailers. Quite sizeable craft for a port with no harbour! The cobles of those days were similar to those of today - 25' long, 5' broad, flat bottomed, 1 to 2 tons burthen, and carrying one mast stepped with a single lug sail. Here again, we find a link with our Viking past, in the inherited shape of the coble, with its high bow, broad curved beam, and overlapping planking. Vessels so constructed are 'clinker built', with the timbers overlapping in the manner of roof slates on a house - which in some areas are also called 'clinkers', hence the derivation.

The larger boats most probably caught more than just fish, for anti-smuggling laws of the mid 1820s included one that prohibited vessels of a 'useful' size being rigged as a lugger (generally accepted as a fast-sailing rig), and any found contravening this law were to be broken up. This law applied to vessels over fifty tons burthen, unless they were licensed. The licence clearly stated the limits within which they may navigate. The Boat Masters of Robin Hood's Bay put in an application for relief, as the law would then prevent them being used in the deep water herring fishery. The Customs Board agreed that any vessel of that size already in use at the time of the passing of the law, which were 'intended for the purpose of fishing' may so be licensed. A satisfactorily useful outcome for the Bay men!

Prior to that, the First 'Hovering' Act, passed in 1718, declared that any vessel under fifty tons, found laden with suspect goods, and 'hovering' or, as we should say nowadays, 'loitering with intent', within two leagues of the coast, was liable to seizure.

Amongst the fishing fraternity it was no secret that on occasions a mere pretence was made at fishing as a means of hoodwinking the authorities. Vessels capable of sailing well out to sea would leave on the evening tide, ostensibly for the fishing grounds beyond the horizon, where they would shoot their nets so as to have a legitimate reason for being there. In time, some of them became so blatantly impudent that they became careless of the dangers. The Authorities, not liking to be made fools of, were compelled to take action against those who were making a good living far too easily, and in 1773, the Admiralty appointed Captain Burrish of the 'Blandford' and Sir Roger Butler of the 'Bonetta' to cruise between Newcastle and Flamborough as part of a scheme to suppress smuggling on this stretch of the coast.

It soon became evident that it was impossible to control the 'goings on' in Robin Hood's Bay from the Whitby base, so a Revenue boat with a crew of six armed men and a 'sitter' or coxwain was established in the village. No doubt a few well laid plans had to be hastily rearranged, but as the Preventives had, of necessity, to be recruited from far afield, and were replaced as soon as they became familiar with the place, so as not to be tempted by bribes, they were perhaps less effective than had been hoped.

As late as 1841, there was still a Preventive force in the village, though now they had taken on a new role as 'Coastguards' - a force formed by the Prince Regent in 1822. The census return for 1841 gives us their names, ages and places of residence. It is interesting to note that several were born in either Scotland or Ireland. How long they each remained here is hard to discover, but it can't have been easy for their wives and children living in such a close and alien community. The Coastguard Officer, Patrick MaCarthy, aged 35, born in Ireland, as was his wife Bridget and two of his five children, lived out at Stoupe Brow, where his house would give a good view of the Bay in both directions. Of his crew members, two - John Smith aged 53, and James Whitton (born in Scotland), lived in the Dock, with his family. James Booker - 50, lived on Fisherhead, James Green aged 40 (also Irish born) lived on Covet Hill, and Michael Hargyn aged 39 (again Irish born) and William Key aged 58, both lived in King Street with wives and daughters.

A living link with the past remains outside the Old Smuggler's Cafe (formerly known as The Ship Launch) in Baxtergate, Whitby, where the now very battered figurehead is all that remains of a French smuggling lugger that was captured in the early 1800s. To prevent the vessel being used again in unlawful trading, she was cut into three parts, then sold to a ship builder in Larpool woods. Her timbers were used to lengthen and convert a local fishing yawl, the 'Thomas and Ann' into a schooner, the old French figure head being given to the yawl's owner, a Mr. Bovill. He was also the owner of the Old Ship Launch (then known as The Exchange) and decided it would make a good decoration. Eventually, the figurehead of the old lugger gave its name to the adjoining passage way of 'Loggerhead's Yard'. The building is reputed to have been a regular meeting place for smugglers - certainly it is well situated, with an entrance door in a passage from which hasty exit could be made in two directions - a quick entry into Baxtergate or an escape into the harbour.

The earlier type of lugger had the foremast stepped well towards the bow, and there was not a great deal of difference in the height of the masts, which were tall enough to carry a topsail.

In light weather, a running bowsprit carried a jibsail. One of the great advantages of the lugger rig was that it enabled the vessel to sail closer to the wind than normal, and when the topsails and jib were set, the lugger thus rigged could easily outdistance the Revenue cutters, despite their enormous spread of canvas. The hulls were frequently constructed from pine wood, rather than the much heavier traditional ship-building timber, oak, from which the Revenue boats were built. This lightness of construction added to the increased speed.

Another advantage was that there were so many alike that it was only with great difficulty that they could be distinguished from one another, and thus definitely identified as being involved in illegal activities.

It is important to realise the amount of shipping activity which was carried on in this area at the time in question. In 1702, Whitby was the sixth largest ship-owning port in England, with a hundred and ten vessels. There were also large numbers of smaller ships of various kinds owned at the fishing villages along the coast. Some, the larger sloops and luggers, were of a size which earned large profits for their owners when engaged in smuggling. Some were especially adapted for the purpose, with false linings to the decks and hulls, where contraband could be very conveniently and safely hidden. On one captured vessel, thirty pounds of tea were discovered in the false floor of the ship's dog kennel!

In addition to the sloops and luggers, the collier brigs which regularly sailed the North Sea between the Tyne and the Thames were useful carriers - ostensibly going about their legitimate business, they frequently transported cargoes of tobacco under the coals! One such, the 'Richard', was wrecked in a gale off Robin Hood's Bay on 3 October 1786. Fortunately all hands were saved, but the cargo was lost.

*The collier brig 'Richard', wrecked in a gale
off Robin Hood's Bay on 3rd October 1786*

11

This, then, was the Robin Hood's Bay of the eighteenth century, the people who formed the core of the smuggling community, and the vessels they used.

So why did these ostensibly honest and hard working folk, tucked away in this remote corner of the world, suddenly appear to change into a ruthless gang of law-breakers? The reason was simple, and one that has attracted Man ever since Eve tempted Adam with that first Golden Delicious: a bit of extra cash!

Yorkshire men - and women - are notoriously canny, and the old Tykes' motto 'hear all, see all, say nowt; eat all, sup all, pay nowt; and if ivver thi does owt fer nowt, allus do it fer thisen' is a pretty direct summing up of the shrewd Yorkshire nature! Added to the fact that no one ever pays taxes willingly, in all generations the art of 'tax dodging' seems to be an acceptable game in many circles. (There is, of course, a subtle and legal difference between tax avoidance and tax evasion). The hard toilers of the eighteenth century certainly had an eye to the main chance when, because of their perfect geographical situation, the opportunity arose to become involved in the secret import of taxable goods, with its enormously tempting but risky profits.

Skippers of smuggling vessels could easily earn £250 for a single night's run; the seamen and overland carriers £5, and the landers on the beach a guinea (£1.05) each - and, remembering the relative increase in the value of money today, these were, in those far off days, huge amounts, way above the normal legitimate earning capacity. No wonder men - and women - were tempted!

The main goods involved were mostly luxury items, such as rum, brandy, expensive wines, and gin for the rich man's wine-cellar; tea and coffee for his drawing room; perfumes, silks, velvets and laces with which to indulge his peacock taste for high fashion; tobacco and snuff, playing cards and chocolate to while away his idle moments; and spices to perk up his sometimes dubious menu!

The list of dutiable goods was endless - by 1815, believe it or not, over 1400 different commodities were taxed!

All these should have been the source of large amounts of revenue for the Government of the time - desperately needed to pay for the numerous European wars in which England was involved in the eighteenth century, but much of the profit never reached the Treasury in London, being secreted instead in dark holes in old sea-coast cottages, ready for a 'rainy day'.

The local populace decided that if the rich were going to indulge, the 'profits' may just as well go into the pockets of the 'deserving poor' as to the Government, especially as the never ending wars were pretty unpopular, and fine principles were thrown aside by those who were in the favourable geographical position of being able to 'cream off' at source.

Napoleon also turned a blind eye to the misplaced loyalties of the 'free traders'; England and France were supposed to be at war, but so much English gold was forthcoming for sales of contraband - some of the rowing boats which traded across the Channel were even known as 'guinea boats' - that he instructed that the French Channel ports be kept open for business. Some free traders earned even more money by selling secrets about the movement of British troops, so Napoleon found them especially useful.

Vast amounts of money were involved; for example, one pound of tea, costing 7d (just less than 3p) in Holland, sold legally in Great Britain for 24s (£1.20p); a gallon of brandy had a total duty of 5s. 2d (26p) - about a week's wages for a working man. Tobacco also saved about 5s. per pound, so there were plenty of customers willing to take risks for the black market goods; in fact, the trade potential was so great that in France and Holland distilleries went into special production of spirits solely for the smuggling market - at a distillery near Amsterdam, in 1779, almost four million gallons of gin were produced, mainly for the

English smuggling trade! This gin could be bought for 1s. a gallon, and sold for up to 6s. - a nice little mark up. Cheap liquor so flooded the market, that gin drinking became a serious social problem.

For some local people, the money earned from the proceeds was their only income. A Customs Officer reported to his superiors in a letter dated 1783; 'Very great quantities of prohibited goods have been run by a great number of armed men, many of whom follow no employment but this illicit practice'. This is borne out by a report in the Newcastle Chronicle for 23 December, 1769: 'The smuggling trade was never carried on to so great an extent as at present. The great number of people that daily attend the coast (and who seem to have no other employ but to carry off the goods) is almost incredible. In spite of the activity of the Revenue Officers and the making of several seizures, it does not appear possible to suppress the trade unless a sufficient number of cutters with experienced Commanders, are stationed off the coast at proper distances.'

A Parliamentary Commission in 1745 stated that of the four million pounds weight of tea consumed in Britain each year, three million pounds had been smuggled in without duty. From the above figures, a quick calculation gives us the amount of well over £3 million being lost in revenue each year....and in those days that was a lot of money.

Some goods attracted two separate taxes; Customs Duty which was paid (or should have been) on entry to the country - this had been in force since Roman times - and Excise Duty, an internal sales tax still in force today, though it was originally introduced in 1664 as a purely temporary tax to help pay for the Civil War.

Although smuggling was at its height in the eighteenth century, the beginnings of the trade can be traced back to 1275 when wool smuggling - 'woolling' or 'owling' - began, to counteract the ban put on its export by Edward I who, realising the potential wealth to be gained from sheep farming, wished to establish an efficient woollen manufacturing industry in England. The products of our British sheep evidently deserved the 'woolmark' even in those days. The use of wool as a symbol of wealth is still in existence even today - the Speaker of the House of Commons sits upon 'the woolsack'. The smuggling fraternity saw the means of earning an extra 'bob' or two - or should it be 'groat' or two - but became over-greedy, and Edward put his royal foot down firmly. We were still in the days when the King ruled in more than name only: the reigning monarch really governed, and passed laws which made illegal export a crime, punishable by imprisonment. Also, as a permanent reminder of one's folly in getting caught in the act, the culprit's right hand was severed, and nailed up on a post as a nasty warning to others. The Government authorised the search of all vessels trading between Scarborough and Berwick-on-Tweed 'as it is said that merchants and others daily ship by stealth in the counties of Northumberland and York, wool, hides, and other merchandise liable to Custom, and export the same without satisfying the King'.

It is perhaps an interesting diversion to note that Geoffrey Chaucer, author of the famous 'Canterbury Tales' was appointed by Edward III in 1374 as Comptroller of Customs and Subsidy of wool, skins, and leather in the Port of London. The wool tax remained chargeable until 1844. An Act of Parliament in 1698 made it illegal for stocks of shorn wool to be kept anywhere near the coast, and all sheep farmers living within five miles of the coast must register with the Customs and keep strict records of all transactions concerning sheep and wool sales.

One good local story relates how the Captain of one of the regular smuggling luggers - possibly the notorious 'Stoney' Fagg of the 'Kent' - (of whom more later) - arrived in the Bay one night, just as dusk was falling. He unloaded his inward cargo of brandy and lace without problem, and had expected to see a fleet of local cobles returning with his pre-arranged 'export' cargo of sheeps' wool. Darkness had fallen and the Captain paced his deck impatiently, scanning the empty expanse of sea and shore with some anxiety. Not wishing to hang around too long for fear of risking capture, nor yet willing to raise anchor and return to France with empty holds, he called to be rowed ashore to investigate. The farmer, who lived somewhere up on Brow Side, was somewhat surprised to be disturbed at his supper, by an angry thumping on the farmhouse door. Not expecting the vessel until the following week, he had not had the sheep sheared and the fleeces neatly tied up in bundles ready for 'export'. A hasty and irate discussion took place, and the only decision made that would satisfy all parties. Onlookers on the shore that night would have been startled to hear a cacophony of bleating, and trampling hooves, as the entire flock of sheep was bundled unceremoniously down the cliff, across the beach to the waiting cobles and ferried out to the lugger for their unexpected trip to the continent! No doubt the farmer would be so busy with all the excitement of this unplanned exploit, that he would have completely forgotten how he was going to account for the disappearance of his flock! When Josiah Clarke, the local constable of Bay Town at that time, made his regular visit out to the farm to check the sheep record, the books would have to be well and truly 'cooked' - alright, the disappearance of a few sheep due to natural causes of disease, or getting stuck in the many bogs on the moorland could be accepted - but to lose an entire flock was just too careless to be true!

16

1,2,3.'The romantic name of Robin Hood's Bay draws visitors from world wide to delight in its unique beauty, explore its quaint streets and lose themselves in its timeless past.'

From that relatively minor misunderstanding, it can be realised that a full smuggling 'run', from its start on the Continent, to its finish in some elegant Regency drawing room, had to run with the smoothness of the wheels of a well-oiled clock. No bad timing, no running down of the workings when someone forgot to wind it up, and especially no loud chiming at the wrong times! A complete run involved a large number of people, who we can imagine linked together as a strong and complete chain. Should one link break under pressure, then all could be lost, and a great many people put at risk. The producers of the spirits on the Continent, or the procurers of the taxable goods, formed the first link in the 'chain'. Secondly came the carriers, such as Captains of the trading vessels, many of whom were ruthless, swashbuckling buccaneers like the infamous 'Smoker' Browning or the notorious 'Stoney' Fagg. The third and fourth links were the landers and storers - the stalwart Bay folk and their colleagues all along the coast, along with the 'tubmen' (who carried the smaller tubs on slings across their shoulders), and the 'batmen' employed to protect them by driving off attackers with 'bats' - hefty iron-tipped poles around five feet in length and useful for poking unwelcome men off horses! These two categories were usually employed on a casual basis, during which time they could earn ten to twelve shillings per night. Fifth in the chain the local farmers and landowners, who put their pack ponies and farm horses and carts on a bit of overtime to transport the goods over the dangerous moorland, to link up with the sixth group, the dealers in the country towns who finally spirited - if that's the right word - the goods into the spotless hands of the landed gentry, who poured the brandy into their cut-glass decanters, gave the perfume to their silk-clad, lace-bedecked wives, and acknowledged their appreciation of the receipt of these little pleasures of life with the odd gold sovereign or two. Silence was, definitely, golden!

All links in the chain held their own potential dangers, but the one that concerns us most here in twentieth century Robin Hood's Bay, was the part played by the landers and storers. We have already established that these were brave and crafty men and women, their sound knowledge of the moods of the sea standing them in good stead, a practical understanding of the prevailing currents, tides, and treacherous rocks being essential for the safe retrieval of contraband dropped overboard during the hours of darkness from a visiting 'delivery' vessel.

If tides or weather conditions were unfavourable for landing onto the beach, or a larger vessel needed to discharge cargo in deeper waters, barrels or packets well wrapped in waterproof oilskins could be lowered over the side on long ropes, anchored with stones, and the position marked with, what was to the eye of the innocent bystander, merely a fishing float. Tubs of spirits took no harm when roped together and dropped overboard in a similar manner to laying a line of lobster pots, weighted with stones or iron bars to make them sink. Tea, however, had to be well wrapped in oiled waterproof skin bags, which were more difficult to sink successfully, needing heavier weights to prevent them bobbing conspicuously to the surface! Corks were used for intermediate floats, but the buoys at either end of a fleet of crab pots or a long line were, in those days, made from tanned dogskin, inflated like a bladder. Did the popular press of the day report the mysterious disappearance of family pets for sinister purposes, one wonders?

Occasionally, perhaps after a storm, an anchoring rope would break, and the contraband float embarrassingly ashore. One story tells how a barrel was spotted floating in on the tide near Mill Beck. Sharp eyes and keen wits passed the message, and very quickly the barrel was salvaged and taken into a nearby smuggler farmer's kitchen. Rejoicing that the contents were, as he suspected, excellent quality rum, and being a generous minded

4. *The author's model smuggler's house, showing many
of the secret hiding places for contraband.*

5,6,7. *The coble (above l.) owes its design to its Viking ancestors. (above r.) Old Smugglers figurehead, Baxtergate, Whitby. (below) 'Bay cottages are built into and on top of one another to a greater extent than anywhere on the Yorkshire coast'.*

fellow, he summoned his friends to a 'bottle party' - the difference being that they arrived with empty bottles and departed with full ones! Unfortunately, Customs Officers were spotted taking a nice evening stroll along the cliffs in the direction of the farmhouse! The rest of the barrel was quickly emptied into a milk churn, filled up with water, and tightly re-bunged. The party goers left discreetly by the back door, and the farmer was discovered scratching his head and looking at the barrel in a puzzled fashion. Importantly, the Customs Officials recorded their find in their notebooks, and ceremoniously removed the barrel to headquarters in Whitby, where the contents were found to be disappointing, to say the least!

Dodges and disguises were manifold, and the canny Yorkshire imagination stretched to its full potential. Innocent-looking objects revealed a wealth of surprising secrets; who would guess that if a certain length of manilla hawser was cut into, it would present the lucky finder with a plug of tobacco? An old scrap of rope lying on the deck looked innocent enough - from the outside - but the smoker had to be sure he'd got the right stuff in his pipe - smouldering tarred rope could be a bit pungent!

Who would guess that the apples delivered to a fruiterer in Whitby were really small bundles of lace, tightly packed into little round boxes, carved and cleverly painted to resemble the fruit? These were brought in by the 'St. Francis', sailing from Gravelines under the command of the French Captain Jean Baptiste La Motte.

Who would guess that the barrels of salt used for curing fish - (once they had duty paid, for until 1825 salt was a taxable commodity, too) - contained a far more valuable cargo tucked away in the centre? A load of these barrels of salt were stored in a warehouse whose floorboards overhung a wooden staithe in Whitby harbour. A cunning smuggler rowed underneath in the middle of the night with brace and bit in his toolbag, and carefully and accurately drilled upwards into the barrels, syphoning off the brandy inside!

Who would guess that the very pregnant-looking fisherwife was not in imminent danger of giving birth in the street, but that her 'bulge' was caused by a variety of packages tucked under her skirts? One such lady caused the local Preventive man in Robin Hood's Bay considerable concern, and he kindly advised her to return home and take to her bed before anything happened! If he had examined her more closely, he could have discovered that not only had she a bottle of gin, a bladder of brandy, a box of coffee, and a pouch of tobacco concealed under her dress, but down her front, a bottle of perfume, exquisite Valenciennes lace 'bandages' under her woolly stockings, and even, perhaps, a tea bag under her bonnet.

8,9,10. *The author in smuggler's costume, and displaying hidden contraband.*
(below) Closely built houses in King Street had adjoining cupboards for passing goods.

In his poem, Rudyard Kipling warns against tampering with any suspicious packages discovered in the bushes, and folks' natural fear of the supernatural was played on to some extent, to warn prying eyes away from vital places. Smugglers often made up tales of ghosts and apparitions to keep away the curious, and the superstition of never picking up a bag found at a crossroads gave those 'in the know' a safe pick-up point. Mind you, if you picked up the wrong bag by mistake, your days were definitely numbered......a traditional cure for convulsions involved binding parings from the nails, together with hair clipped from the crown of the head, in a cloth along with a half-penny. The bag was then set down at a crossroads, and whoever picked it up would 'pick up' the disease - so, naturally, any suspicious package could fairly safely be left there. Lonely crossroads were also the traditional burial grounds of suicides and murderers - spooky places at the best of times, even in broad daylight!

Playing on the fear of ghosts and death gave the smuggling fraternity opportunity to indulge in a few bizarre tricks and ruses: one quick-thinking Bay man turned a potential disaster into an hilarious entertainment for his colleagues, although, in the telling of the tale, he had to admit his own shortcomings. Due to take over watch duty in the early morning hours on the night 'Jenny was coming' (one of the warning catchphrases that a run was imminent) he unfortunately overslept, and on waking and realising his error, bundled his long white nightshirt into his baggy trousers, hastily pulled on his dark gansey, and rushed out to his post. Blocking his way on the cliff path, most inconveniently, was the Preventive officer. With a chuckle, the late sleeper stripped off his gansey, pulled out his nightshirt, and with silent, gliding steps and outstretched flapping arms, crept up behind the unsuspecting Preventive. In a sepulchral voice he intoned "It's a fine night for the dead to be walking abroad!" The Preventive's blood froze in his veins, his hair stood on end, and he fled, leaving the watchkeeper alone on the cliff, free to carry out his duties.

Another macabre tale tells of one who escaped capture by feigning death. A warrant had been issued for this man's arrest on charges of smuggling. His wife was the local layer-out, and she practised her art so skilfully on her still living husband, that the arresting officer, finding her grief stricken, took one look in the coffin in the dark corner of the room, offered his condolences, and promptly tore up the warrant. The 'corpse' lay low for a few days before making a miraculous recovery!

Stories pass down from generation to generation, and inbuilt superstitions die hard - even today some local people still suppress a shiver when walking up Lingers Hill, in case they encounter 'Lingers ghost' emerging round a corner. A white-sheeted figure riding a white horse frequently 'appeared' in the area when, a smuggling run being due, it was desirable to keep this particular part of the route clear of inquisitive snoopers!

This short section of the 'main' road, between Robin Hood's Bay and the neighbouring village of Fylingthorpe, linked two lonely country tracks leading from the back of Robin Hood's Bay through to open moorland, and being near the beginning of a pack-pony 'run' was the most exposed part of the route.

A last story concerns one of the many fake funerals that took place country wide - showing the elaborate extent to which smugglers were willing to go to land the goods. A parson, new to the area, was summoned out to a ship anchored in the Bay, to give the last rites to a supposedly dying sailor. Of course, he 'died' shortly after the priest left, and the burial, having been pre-arranged for early the next morning before the ship sailed on her way, the coffin, containing no sad corpse, but a man's weight of contraband, was duly shipped ashore and buried with quiet and sorrowful dignity by his shipmates. Within twenty-four hours, the ship had sailed beyond the horizon, the new grave robbed,

'Linger's Ghost': a local farmer, wearing a white sheet and riding a white horse patrolled the stretch of road between Robin Hood's Bay and Fylingthorpe on the nights when a smuggling run was due.

and yet another run of goods was on its way to the drawing rooms of the gentry.

Some of the contraband may not have had very far to travel: a highly successful local smuggling syndicate was led by Squire Farsyde of Thorpe Hall in Fylingthorpe, and the eccentric Doctor Richard Willis who lived high on the cliffs at Raven Hall. (He achieved fame - and notoriety - by being the physician who treated the madness of King George III, introduced hypnosis as a cure for insomnia at a guinea a time, and squandered his fortune on racing lice!)

His remote cliff-top eyrie, six hundred feet above sea level, gave him an unsurpassed view of the coastline and its activities: in the spectacular gardens which he created by blasting out the cliff, he cut out a little square chamber for hiding a signaller with a lantern.

As evening falls, and the moon casts its silvery light over the glimmering Bay, the intense silence that pervades this lonely place captures the perfect atmosphere in which to sit and let the imagination recreate the events of the past. A keen ear and a sharp eye may one night discern shadowy figures stealthily moving across Beastcliff in search of the large haul of contraband which, local legend tells, is still there, unclaimed for over two hundred years.

Considering that a full 'run' involved so many 'links' in the chain, it was sometimes necessary for contraband to be stored until the arrangements for transport and disposal were in place, and here again, ingenuity had full rein, and the peculiarities of traditional Bay architecture came into their own. Imagination can run riot, and the romantic heart beat wildly at the discovery of a creaky floorboard, a sliding panel, or a loose brick or stone in the wall when an old cottage is being renovated. Many of these could well have concealed the odd secret in the past, and who is to deny the fact two hundred years later? Let the doubt remain, and leave the old memories in place, to be mulled over and debated by the firesides of the present day occupants.

From time to time, however, more definite signs are uncovered; a few years ago, still in existence, was a sliding panel at the back of a cottage cupboard which led straight into the pub next door! Very handy on a cold winter's night if the gentleman of the house fancied a pint! Such links between the closely packed Bay cottages enabled contraband to pass from house to house, from the bottom of the Bank to the top, without ever emerging into daylight. Not only the close juxtaposition of the cottages, but the steepness of the streets, and the fact that much of the village was built into the sides of a ravine, added to the irregularities of the architecture. By frequently having front and back doors not only at varying floor levels, but exiting onto different streets, made hurried escapes puzzling, head-scratching affairs for the Revenue men. A recent renovation of some old properties in Whitby revealed two-hundred-year-old ropes still hanging in the chimneys. These would have been used, not only for storing contraband in the smoky recesses, but for emergency escape routes, either from the Excise men or Press Gang. Up the chimney the fugitive would go, hand over hand, trying not to give the game away by coughing and choking - cross over at the top, and down the other side to exit by a neighbour's fireplace and dash away down the narrow network of alleyways. Santa Claus was not the only one to arrive down the chimney covered in soot!

The wide ingle-nooks of those days also housed concealed platforms for hiding places. The Old Smuggler's Cafe, formerly the Old Ship Launch in Baxtergate, Whitby, still has one of these. Loose hearth stones with hollows underneath, cavities in walls, and trap doors placed under large and heavy pieces of furniture may all have one day played their part in an exciting and dangerous 'game'.

Legend has it that a murder victim is buried under the hearthstone of a famous nearby moorland inn. Combined with the superstition that extreme ill luck would fall on the person who extinguished the peat fire that had burned continuously in that fireplace for nigh on a hundred years, ensured that here for sure was a safe hiding place for anyone willing to take the risk!

Occasionally, a true story of the supernatural emerges. In this case, the haunted cupboard in question, although ideal for concealing contraband because of its reputation, may, due to the authenticity of its incredibly sad story, never have been put to use. The house, although known to many local people, has, for reasons of privacy, not been identified in this book.

The property belonged to a widowed sea captain, the father of a young daughter somewhere between the ages of seven and twelve years old. During his absence, the girl was left in the care of a relative in another village. Sad at the thought of her father's lengthy and distant voyaging, and having already taken a clinging and tearful farewell, the thought of parting became unbearable, and, unbeknown to the sea captain, she followed at a safe distance as he returned home to collect his last minute belongings. Silently she crept up the stairs behind him, but on hearing his booted feet tramp across his bedroom floor and unexpectedly begin to descend the staircase, fearing discovery she slipped into an open cupboard and hid in the dark recess until the footsteps had passed. Noticing the door slightly ajar, he snecked it closed, turned the key in the lock, hurried downstairs, locked the front door, pocketed his key, and started away on his journey.

The child's terrified cries and frantic knockings went unheeded in the empty house, and gradually faded as she grew weaker. Not until the father's return several months later, was the pathetic little body discovered, still clinging to the inside door knob.

Twentieth century workmen in the house have been chilled to the marrow on hearing faint knockings, and sensitive visitors have even heard the child's unheeded cries as she sobbed her way into oblivion.

Smuggling was a great 'leveller' of age and social class - all were tarred with the same brush - fishermen, innkeepers, landed gentry, and clergy; mind you, all of them would have been horrified at the suggestion that they were involved in anything underhand or illegal. 'All's fair in love and war', so goes the saying; certainly they all considered it was a fair game, and the main complaint against the Preventives was that 'they hindered many a poor body getting an honest living'! The local squires put up considerable finance, and formed syndicates which bought or hired vessels purely for smuggling purposes - and became extremely wealthy from the proceeds.

A contemporary journal of 1774 reported 'the practice of smuggling increases amazingly in these parts. It is become so general that seizures are almost daily made and many people of good circumstances are known to deal largely in that pernicious trade. If this contraband traffic is suffered to go on it will inevitably drain this country of a great part of its money and endanger the lives and morals of numbers of its inhabitants.'

Age was no barrier, either; from small child to aged grandparent, all could be involved to some degree. Who would suspect that the golden-haired child, thumb in innocent mouth, peaceful in rosy-cheeked slumber, was laid upon a mattress full of tea and tobacco; that the lump under the quilted coverlet was not a favourite doll but a small keg of rum; that the cupboards under the box bed were stuffed full of illicit goods, and that the white haired grandmother, sitting by the nursery fire with her knitting, was comfortably dozing and gently smiling at reminiscences of her wily cunning.

For this grandmother had a tale to tell......

One night, a considerable cargo of spirits had been successfully run ashore, and most of it stowed away, when the Preventive man put in an unexpected and unwelcome appearance. The smugglers moved fast in the darkness, muffled boots echoed dully on the cobblestones, and suddenly, old Rebecca's door burst open, letting in an icy blast of air and a feeling of urgent panic.

A keg of brandy was heaved unceremoniously through the door and dumped at her feet, a gruff voice ordering her to get rid of it - quick! The door banged shut, gusting the smoke from the fire in a choking cloud, and Rebecca took stock of the situation. Quick thinking was called for; no time to shift the furniture and lower the barrel into the cellar. Rolling it beside the fire, she upended it, picked up her knitting, and, spreading her skirts wide round her somewhat uncomfortable seat, prepared for the anticipated visit of the Preventive man. She had not long to wait before, with a peremptory knock, her door burst open again to reveal the tall dark-cloaked figure in tricorne hat, his stern features illuminated by the rays of a horn lantern. The old lady bravely sat tight, stoically denying any knowledge of the illicit spirit. The excuse that she could not accompany him on his inspection due to her severe rheumatism preventing any unwarranted movement was accepted. The 'Sniv' searched alone, but found nothing. As the door closed behind him, after a curt "Goodnight!", old Rebecca put down her knitting, stretched her back with a sigh of relief, and got up with a smile of satisfaction. She'd outwitted him! A brave action, for even at her advanced age, punishment may not have been avoided.

The fact that the women folk at 'Bay were just as deeply involved in the smuggling trade as men, contributed greatly to the success of the operations. Truly the saying that 'behind every successful man is a good woman' was more than appropriate here!

Of doubtful authenticity as a hiding and landing place is the tunnel which leads from beside the slipway to the beach, running back under the main street, to emerge under 'The Little House' in the ravine just below the old Wesleyan Chapel. The tunnel is reputed to date back to about 1550, and is believed to have been constructed to culvert King's Beck to allow more properties to be built on the top. It was well made, with solid arching all along its length. Building space being scarce, this seems likely, but it may quite possibly have had a secondary use in the smuggling activities. It was certainly extremely handily situated, so why not? The smuggling fraternity would hardly ignore its potential usefulness, nor be put off by its other use as a drain. What was a bit of unpleasantness when so much was at stake? The branch tunnel which runs under what is now Bligh's Restaurant, along Albion Road, and under the Congregational Hall is recorded as being the escape route of the crew of a lugger, chased by Customs officers. A low, wet and uncomfortable escape into the dank recesses of Marna Dale but a safe hiding place in the lonely country beyond - better than capture and impressment into the navy. Other tunnels on Stoupe Brow may also have been useful - one a drain for the old alum works in the cliffs reputedly had a link leading to the cellar of Stoupe Brow Cottage; the alum workers up in the quarries were also involved in the landing and disposal of run goods.

Recent surveys have exposed blocked-up passageways, which previously led from - or to! - the properties immediately above. One appeared to lead directly to the old Fisherman's Arms in the Dock, and another to the old Nag's Head pub. It was also possible that these two, meeting in the main tunnel almost opposite each other, could easily have been a useful subterranean link between the buildings. The public houses were well known to be involved in the smuggling activities......in fact they featured in a somewhat exciting drama which rocked the village in

a,b,c. Some of the village's hidden tunnels. (above l.) Entrance to King's Beck tunnel from Chapel Street. (above r.) King's Beck tunnel from Wayfoot. (below) Marna Dale tunnel, under Albion Road, witnessed the escape of a lugger's crew.

October 1779. It was rumoured that some two hundred kegs of brandy had been landed on the beach, 'spirited' into the tunnel, and thence, through the slimy route up the passage or drain, into the cellar of the 'Fisherman's Arms' in the Dock. This building, dating back to 1680, later the home of Oliver Storm, the last 'Bay lifeboat coxwain and now a holiday cottage, may well have had such a link with the subterranean world. The local version of the story (you will read the Customs and Excise's own version shortly) is that as the last of the two hundred kegs were being stored, the Preventive men, backed up by the Dragoons who were stationed here at the time - got wind of the operation and put in an unexpected and unwelcome appearance. A short and violent fight broke out, in which the Dragoons outnumbered and overpowered the local men. Two of the soldiers were deputed to keep guard over the haul. It was cold, damp and dark in the cellar, and long hours of waiting stretched ahead through the night. During the fighting, one of the barrels was cracked and had started to leak. A dark stain spread gradually and pungently across the dry wood of the damaged cask. Slowly and tantalisingly the appetising liquid dripped onto the sandy floor of the cellar.

The bored Dragoons, hypnotised by the regular drip...drip...drip of the oozing brandy, shivered as the clammy, ice-cold atmosphere crept into their bones. They yawned, and as their gaping mouths closed, they caught each other's eyes. The yawn turned into a grin, and with a broad wink, one of them stood, stretched painfully, and disappeared up the long flight of stone steps into the bar room of the pub. All was quiet; the publican was fast asleep, the last of his customers long since gone to their beds. Reaching out for a couple of glasses, the officer retraced his steps to the cellar, and holding out the glass, caught the slowly dripping liquid which gleamed richly golden in the flickering light of the single candle.

Impatience overtook his companion, and, reaching for his sword, he rammed the point into the crack, twisting it to widen the gap - out gushed the brandy in generous quantities. A gift from the gods! Toasting each other, feeling the warmth of the spirit penetrating to the very depths of their aching bones, they drank again, and deeply, until the silent night grew merry with their bawdy songs and raucous laughter. Up above, in the moonlit street, a passing fisherman returning late home to his bed - no doubt having been busy on his own account elsewhere - heard the merriment down below, and, guessing what had happened, hastened quietly to rouse his companions. In no time at all, the Dock was full of smirking, whispering, jostling navy-jerseyed smugglers; a hail of small pebbles at his bedroom window roused the sleeping innkeeper, who, candle in hand, turned the heavy iron key in the lock and admitted the 'rescue party'. Fingers to lips, they waited until the noisy singing subsided into the loud snores of deep, drugged slumber. Down the stone steps they tiptoed, tied up the unsuspecting guards, and handed the kegs, one by one, out into the street. Within minutes, all two hundred had miraculously vanished into the 'Bay's warren of alleyways with their secret hideouts. Next morning, two very thick-headed soldiers awoke, stiff and very cold, to an embarrassingly empty cellar and the displeasure of their senior officers.

The official report that went in to the Headquarters of the Customs and Excise must have caused a bit of a flurry over the morning coffee (duty paid, one hopes, seeing who was drinking it!). '1779, October 8. We are advised from Whitby that on the 6th instant, Mesrs Harrison, Smith and Boyse, Officers of Excise, seized in the dwelling house of an Innkeeper at Robin Hood's Bay, upwards of two hundred casks of smuggled brandy and geneva, with 150 bags of tea; also a chest in which were blunderbusses and cartouche boxes for twenty men; but immediately the whole was rescued, save 20 casks and 10 bags, by a desperate smugglers crew

*d,e,f. (above l.) The old Alum Works tunnel on Brow Side from the beach. (below l.)
The tunnel entrance. (below r.) Smuggler's signal chamber cut into the rock at Ravenscar.*

commanded by the noted Dover, who some time before, broke into the Custom House at Hartlepool. Much to the honour of Captain Barnes, commanding a party of Cumberland Militia at Whitby, he being acquainted with the affair, detached a serjeants guard to the officers assistance. Upwards of 20 of the said crew had paraded the town of Robin Hood, completely equipped with firearms, threatening death and destruction to all their opposers; but on hearing of the Militia they fled in the most precipitate manner, leaving blunderbusses, swords and pistols behind them, and in some of the blunderbusses were no fewer than 20 balls.'

Of course, not every night was so exhaustingly exciting, but it is perhaps significant to pause a moment to consider the impact of the intensity of the operations.

'Old Fisherman's Arms' dating back to 1680.

From the 'official' report of the Fisherman's Arms debacle, it can be seen that the smugglers did not have everything their own way all the time, although bribes and threats were frequently used to persuade the 'Snivs' (as the Preventive Men were derogatively called) to turn a blind eye. A crude and illiterate letter was thrust rudely through the door of a Customs Officer's house in Coatham, near Redcar, in December 1774, one which was most likely similar to those threats issued against the hated blue coated officers all along the coast: 'Damn your Ise if we don't smash your Brains out. You may as well take what we give you, as other officers do, and if you don't well sware that you take 'bribes' you had better take them than not. Damn your Ise. Keep off the Sands' (it was probably not signed 'a friend'!)

It may well have been a threatening letter such as this that caused the Riding Officer stationed in 'Baytown in 1773, John Robinson, to waiver in his loyalty to the King. It is a known fact that some of the Preventive men did side with the smugglers and shared in the resulting profits. However, Mr. Robinson may have been just a little too indiscreet, as the postman delivered him a severe letter of rebuke from the Custom Collector at Whitby:-

'A great smuggling at Robin Hood's Town which had been laid before the Board and by their order sent down here and directed a strict enquiry and full report thereon. As you and Mr. Forster are represented to be greatly concerned therein, you are therefore to make a full reply in regard to the smuggling trade at Robin Hood's Bay and also what is alleged against you for concerning, encouraging and receiving gratification for permitting the pernicious trade, as soon as you possibly can that the affair may be speedily laid before the Board'.

He may have had good reason to 'fall in with the crowd' if conditions were already as bad as suggested the following year:-

A report from the Prevention Officer in Robin Hood's Bay in 1774 stated 'when the weather is favourable, large smuggling vessels are off Robin Hood's Bay with their boats on shore landing goods, the crews of which are become so audacious that the Officers on shore dare not attack them, they so frequently have firearms.'

Another locally based Preventive man, Philip Salmon, became quite upset when his superior officers voiced their suspicions on his loyalty. Salmon owned a trading vessel which was engaged in deliveries up and down the coast - ideal for a bit of personal 'free-trading'. Fortunately for him, on the occasion his ship was searched, nothing untoward was found, and he decided to teach his superiors a lesson.

Eventually he confessed that he had on board a valuable piece of timber on which he had not paid duty. But search as they would, the Customs Officers could not find it anywhere. Salmon sat in his cabin chuckling, putting a final polish to his new wooden leg!

When situations really got the better of the local Revenue department, and defiant smugglers were cocking a too defiant snook at officialdom, running rings around the lone Constable of Bay Town - (in the 1770's Josiah or 'Josh' Clarke) - he could always call for assistance in the form of the 2nd Dragoons from York. These were the forerunners of the later famous Scots Greys - highly trained troopers with experience of the famous battlefields of Europe. Blenheim and Malplaquet were a far cry from the wilds of North Yorkshire, but to the six troopers and their sergeant deployed to Robin Hood's Town in 1775, the job of 'assisting in defeating the smugglers' had its small consolations.

Their normal pay of less than a shilling a day was bonussed by an extra 2d, a daily ration of five pints of beer, and a promised share in any prize money from captured contraband. After five pints of beer a day, one wonders at their effectiveness in patrolling the warren of narrow alleyways that make up Bay Town!

g,h,i. Baytown's network of narrow streets made the Preventive Officer's job a hard one! (above l.) Sunnyside led conveniently into the country. (above r.) The Openings. (below) Linger's Corner; locals watched out for the 'ghost' when a smuggling run was due!

j,k,l. (above l.) Martin's Row. (above r.) Moonlight over Ravenscar - an ideal night for running goods ashore. (below) Rough tracks gave access over the moors to smugglers pony trains.

Large war horses were not exactly practical in 'Bay, either, and really all they could do was put in a red-coated appearance as a deterrent. But the wily fishermen knew plenty of landing points other than the slipway, and the homesick Scots, with their broad accents, finding the equally broad Yorkshire speech just as difficult to understand, presumably made the best of their outlandish station, the free beer, and the ozone-laden air!

In 1775, however, probably owing to the strain of the American War of Independence, the Royal North British Dragoons were called away from the coast into foreign service, leaving the way clear for the smuggling which was now practised so openly that 'you cannot go out in the morning or evening without seeing geneva on men or womens' shoulders, or on horseback, or in fish machines.'

In some of the villages a few miles inland, the trading of contraband was carried on quite blatantly. There were established meeting places where goods were sold - 'Gin Garth' and 'Brandy Bridge' near Danby and Castleton could tell a good many tales, could the old stones speak!

One delightful story tells how, one bright moonlight night, a group of country smugglers were surprised by Preventives whilst retrieving contraband, with hay rakes, from its hiding place at the bottom of the village duck pond. They were not the simple-minded yokels they made themselves out to be. When questioned, one chewed reflectively on a length of straw, and scratched his head thoughtfully before replying, slowly and with a hardly concealed twinkle in his eye; "Whoy, we be rakin' moon gold from t'surface o' t'pond. We'm mekkin owersels rich t'noight!"

Violence could erupt at any time. On one occasion, as reported in a newspaper on June 16, 1776, events turned very nasty and murder ensued. What occurred was as follows: 'A smuggling cutter's boat, laden with geneva, went on shore at Runswick. The Officer of the Customs there, with four Privates of the First Regiment of Dragoons, took possession of the boat. The men belonging to her, seeing what had happened, went to the Customs House officer and soldiers, and agreed with them that they should have all the liquor provided they would relinquish the boat, and prevailed on the Dragoons to discharge their pistols, which was no sooner done than the smugglers rose and beat the Dragoons so cruelly that one of them died the next morning. He had been nineteen years in his Regiment and through four campaigns in Germany. The Customs Officer saved himself by flight. A Coroners Jury returned a verdict of 'wilful murder' against the smugglers'. The men were part of the crew of the 'Kent' under the notorious Stoney Fagg and a reward of £100 was offered for their capture. They were taken with the 'Kent' off Filey in July the following year.

Without doubt, the Preventive Men had an awkward and unpleasant job. Even if they made an arrest, it was almost impossible to get a warrant signed, as most of the local magistrates were part of the smuggling fraternity, and convictions of local 'miscreants' extremely difficult to obtain.

What especially annoyed everyone concerned was that, no matter how trivial the charge brought, a person had to prove his innocence - quite a reversal of our present day law of 'innocent until proved guilty'. Many quite innocent people were put to great trouble to satisfy the customs officials. The local magistrates were only too aware of this and rarely convicted a local person if they could reasonably dismiss the case.

This happened in the case of Captain David Pinkney, a Robin Hood's Bay sea captain of some reputation! The local Constable had been 'after him' for some time, but the slippery character had cunningly avoided capture. On 6 January, 1795, a warrant was issued for his arrest for 'obstructing the Officers of the Revenue in their duty'. Underground information had reported that he was 'now at home at Robin Hood's Town and

m,n,o. The face of Baytown has changed due to 'accidents'. (above) A runaway lorry demolished the Old Forge. (below) The landslide in 1780 changed the skyline dramatically - compare this photo with the engraving opposite page 1.

p,q,r. Winter in the Bay. (above l.) high seas batter the cottages as (above r.) winter holds the south shore in its icy grip. (below) Storm clouds gather over Ravenscar.

may be apprehended if proper authority received'. The Town Constable approached his house with some trepidation; Pinkney was a desperate character who would not fall into the authority's hands without a struggle. Having had a 'tip off' as to the warrant, Pinkney had barricaded himself in his house, and met the demands of Josiah Clarke, the Town Constable, with a defiant barrage from his shotgun and an invective of abusive language. Constable Clarke, realising that discretion was the better part of valour, fearing for his life, returned home defeated, and sent the warrant back marked 'Not executed'. In the official report of this fiasco, the Customs officer wrote: 'This we cannot help attributing to the irresolution of the Constable of Robin Hood's Town where Pinkney resides. The latter, on the approach of the Officers to take him, fastened the door of his dwelling house, which the Constable at first doubted the power of the Warrant to authorise him to break open. He afterwards refused to take that step on the grounds that his life would be endangered from the desperate character of the Defendant. Messrs Maxwell and Herbert, the Officers whom Pinkney obstructed, who were with the Peace Officer, did not think themselves at liberty to pursue any measures without his concurrence....The Defendant was on point of going to sea. The earliest intimation will be given so that another Warrant may be issued on his return.'

The fate of Pinkney remains a mystery. Did he return to capture, or did he outwit the Authorities yet again? Customs records appear to leave the case unresolved......yet is the ghost of Captain Pinkney still laughing?

In recent years, a dark cloaked, tricorne hatted figure has been seen on the open balcony at the top of King Street. Is it in the imagination, or is he still heard chuckling at his cleverness?

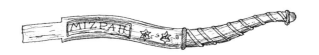

Does the ghost of Captain David Pinkney still appear, watching the horizon for incoming contraband?

One of the highly respected local magistracy gave cause for a good yarn over the pints in the local pub. As already well established, even the most respectable and 'law-abiding' citizens in the district were not entirely innocent, and occasionally got their fingers burnt! One of these respected gentlemen was riding home along a supposedly deserted lane, with a couple of gin tubs slung across his saddle. Round a distant corner approached two uniformed riders - recognisable even at a distance as Officers of His Majesty's Revenue. Quick action called for, the local magistrate slipped from his horse, and dived into the gorse bushes to hide. Not having time to 'unsling' the gin, but only to save his own skin and reputation, he kept a low profile while the horse ambled innocently towards the oncoming riders. Horse and gin were duly captured, the gin impounded in the Customs House, and the horse sent for sale at the next Egton Fair. It being a good horse, and one of which the magistrate was inordinately fond - he had the doubtful pleasure of having to attend the sale and buy the animal back! He was fortunate in being able to do this for a matter of a few pounds, as the tale of the sale had spread like wildfire and caused a great deal of amusement. The magistrate had few competitors bidding against him. The local folk had enjoyed the joke hugely, and who knew when they might appear in front of this very 'beak' on some charge of poaching? He would not have dealt kindly with the new owner of his best horse!

Although the actual landing and storing of contraband was largely the responsibility of the seafaring folk, the job of transporting inland eventually fell to organised groups of horse owners from the farming community or the gentry. Many of these, however, did not wish to be actively involved personally, but were not averse to 'lending' a horse and cart or sledge in return for a small 'recompense'. All the farmer had to do was to ensure the animal required for the night shift had been rested, well fed and watered, was safely in the specified stable with harness readily to hand, along with heavy sacking 'boots' for muffling the hooves, and the sledge or cart placed where it could be utilised without undue noise.

In the morning, along with the returned 'borrowed' horse, a little 'thank you' gift would no doubt be expected, buried in the hayloft or other pre-arranged drop-off point. Thorpe Hall, in Fylingthorpe, the former home of Squire Farsyde, apparently had a stone slab laid in the lawn, which gave access to a concealed chamber underneath. Out of sight of the Squire, it was a case of 'what the eye didn't see', although the Squire was firmly believed to be part of a highly successful local smuggling syndicate, which put up considerable money to finance operations.

In many country districts, a horse found sweating in the stable in the morning was said to have been 'hag-ridden' by witches. From this superstition derives the term 'nightmare', and the use of 'witch stones' with holes in them being hung over the stable door as a deterrent charm. But the question whether the horse had been used for a midnight ride instead of a broomstick, or out on some other nefarious business, was a matter for its owner to decide upon the answer in the morning! Country fear of the supernatural was exploited in the interests of secrecy, and as no right-minded person would risk meeting the local witch on her way back from a midnight excursion, the stables were, therefore, fairly safe ground for smuggling activities.

One of the well-used inland routes led through the Littlebeck valley. The village of Ugglebarnby became a relay station for spirits, tea and tobacco which were brought along the old pannier ways from the coast by teams of pack ponies, the leader of which wore a small tinkling bell to identify it as a contraband train. This was a very reliable pony, surefooted and familiar with all the vagaries of the dangerous route. During the day it was rested, and stabled at a nearby farm, consequently known as 'Tinkler's Hall'. At night, much of the contraband was taken to York on a black mare, which was as difficult to spot on a dark night as the proverbial black cat in the coal cellar!

North Cheek, or "Ness Point" at the north end of the Bay.

That the members of this formerly law-abiding, hard-working community were now completely bitten by the 'smuggling bug' is without question, and that the majority of the population were involved is a certain fact - not to be would cause suspicion, and though not all were violent and bloodthirsty, most of the inhabitants would tend to hold the law in contempt. A workman could earn more from one single packhorse-load of contraband than from a week's honest labour. No true Yorkshireman would throw up such an opportunity! The staunch Church and Chapel-goers had a conscience to wrestle with, and moral principles had a hard fight against the practicalities of earning extra money to provide for the family. 'Charity begins at home' may well have been a favoured text to hang over the mantelpiece in the cliff-edge cottages. A 'Robin Hood' attitude of robbing the rich to give to the poor was undoubtedly prevalent in this aptly named village. However, religious conscience posed a large problem for the famous Methodist preacher, John Wesley, who visited 'Bay eleven times during his ministry. He writes with affection of the simple people of this place, although they caused him a certain amount of heartsearching in their somewhat pigheaded and self-righteous attitudes, some of them being 'very wise in their own eyes', and 'their continued jars with one another prevented their increase in either grace or number'. (In June 1784 they were better behaved - 'At present they seem to be all at peace; so I hope we shall now have joy over them').

John Wesley was bitterly opposed to smuggling - he had spoken out strongly against it just up the coast in Sunderland - and especially down in Cornwall where it was equally rife.

On 16 June 1757, he recorded in his journal that he had 'told them plain, none can stop with us unless he part with all sin, particularly robbing the King, selling or buying run goods, which I could no more suffer than robbery on the highway. This

I enforced on every Member the next day. A few would not promise to refrain so these I was forced to cut off.'

John Wesley had actually opened the new 'preaching house' in Robin Hood's Bay in June 1779 - less than only four months before the incident of the 'Fisherman's Arms' brandy kegs. It is perhaps significant to note that on none of his eleven visits to the 'Bay does he make any reference whatever to smuggling. Perhaps this shows the wisdom of the great man, for if he had spoken out publicly against the evils of smuggling, he may well have lost his entire congregation; for certain, many of them would be 'up to the eyes' in illicit goods, and discreetly he may have had a quiet word on the side! Bay men, sailing to all parts of the globe, were known to be carriers of Wesley's words and preachings - better keep them in favour and ensure they would continue to spread the gospel in foreign parts. But to those who read Wesley's fiery and fearless words to other 'sinning' congregations, his silence in Robin Hood's Bay on a matter of such disfavour, remains something of a mystery, for he was no coward and pulled no punches in his preaching. Normally his 'Bay congregations hung avidly on every word. On Wednesday 24th June, 1761, he wrote in his journal; 'I preached at six in the Lower Street near the quay. In the midst of the sermon a large cat, frightened out of a chamber, leaped down upon a woman's head, and ran over the heads or shoulders of many more; but none of them moved or cried out, any more than if it had been a butterfly.'

In 1772, the Customs and Excise Searcher stationed in 'Baytown, Horatio Roberts by name, had a 'tip off', and went on a 'social call' to the house of William and Mary Cobb.

Some years later, a Mary Cobb of Chapel Street was named as the owner of a 'garden and pig cote' which she donated to the Wesleyan Trustees as building land for enlarging the new Chapel. Is it unreasonable to surmise that Wesley's words may have pricked her conscience, following the following recorded incident?

After a satisfying drink of tea, Horatio Roberts sat at his desk, picked up his quill pen, dipped in the ink pot and began to write his report:-

'Went to the house of William Cobb in Robin Hood's Town about four in the evening. In a lodging room below stairs upon a bed where Cobb and his wife usually lay, found two and a half ankers of geneva, and in which same bed four bags of tea, and in the same room in another place, fourteen bags of tea, and in an unlocked drawer in the next room, six cannisters of tea, and upstairs at the same time in the said house in an open closet, five bags of tea, and in an adjoining chamber in an open closet twelve cannisters and ten single pounds of tea. Cobb himself was at home when the seizure was made, and the wife told the officer she was privy to the goods being lodged there.'

Mary certainly appeared to enjoy her afternoon 'cuppa', although Wesley himself was said to have given up drinking tea as a mark of public protest against smuggling.

John Wesley

Not only did the smuggling fraternity have the Preventives to curb their activities, but it was wise to keep a 'weather eye' open for the sudden arrival of the justly-feared Press Gang. Life in the Royal Navy was nothing short of sheer hell, with death the only final discharge. Admiral Vernon, known as 'Old Grog' from the grogram cloak he habitually wore (this nickname also being applied to the watered down issue of the daily tot of rum which he instigated in 1740) was one of the rare more humane 'top brass', showing some concern for the conditions of the men under his care. 'Our fleets are first manned by violence [a reference to the Press Gang] and maintained by cruelty. When our ships are to be fitted, an impress is sent into the streets, to bring those who fall in the way, by force into the vessels; from that time they are, in effect, condemned to death; since they are never allowed to set foot on shore, but turned over from ship to ship, and when they have finished one expedition, hurried into another, without any regard to the hardships they have undergone, or the length of the voyage; so that they must live upon salt provisions, without their pay, till they shall be consumed by the scurvy or die of some other distemper, which they have contracted by the hardships they have suffered, and the provisions on which they have been obliged to subsist; a practice so horrible and barbarous that it is sufficient to deter anyone from entering the service at all'.

Thus, life was fraught with peril, and it soon becomes obvious to today's historically minded visitor, why the 'Bay was such a good place for subterfuge.

The actual presence of the Press Gang in the village on one occasion, did not, however, deter one ruthless and notorious smuggler known as 'Leatherthumb'. On arrival of his vessel off the 'Bay, a message was sent out that the men dared not emerge from their houses to 'run' his cargo because the Press Gang were in the area. Undeterred, Leatherthumb landed a boat crew and turned them loose in Bay Town, where they fought the Press Gang

11,12,13. (above l.) Thorpe Hall, former home of Squire Farsyde and (r) Raven Hall, home of Dr. Richard Willis, both members of a local smuggling syndicate. From his home on the high cliff top (below) Dr. Willis could keep a keen eye on the 'goings on' across the bay.

off with such violence and viciousness that many were badly wounded and found by the roadside and in ditches, lame and helpless. Leatherthumb and his swashbuckling desperadoes wiped the blood off their swords, spat on their hands, and proceeded to land the goods with impunity!

A typical smuggling lugger, with its lightly constructed hull of pine, and a good spread of sail.

The Preventive men not only had the local inhabitants to contend with, but they and the Riding Officers whose duty was to form a mobile link with the various branches of the Customs and Excise service, had a terrible time getting around due to the conditions of the roads. Frequent complaints went in to the local authority, and in those days seemed to have no more effect than they do today!

A meagre annual pay cheque of £42, out of which the Riding Officer had also to buy and maintain his own horse added to his disgruntlement.

In the eighteenth century, Parishes were responsible for maintaining the highways within their own boundaries. Up to the sixteenth century, very little attention was given to the upkeep of roads and bridges, but things got so bad that in 1555, Queen Mary's Parliament passed the first Statute of Highways, which stipulated that each Parish should elect 'two honest persons yearly' to be surveyors of highways. Each parishioner had to give four days labour on the roads each year, and farmers were obliged to provide horses and carts. In 1774, in the days which concern us for the present subject, the surveyors for the Township of Fylingdales were Henry Ellery and George Cockrill. It was all above board and proper, as they were sworn in by the Whitby magistrates, and during their year of office, collected £18. 19s. 1d. in lieu of Statute Days of work, and £18. 13s. 7d. from Highways Rates. The money was spent in wages to labourers who were paid 18d (=7^1/2 p today) per day, and masons were well paid at 23^1/2d (9 p) daily.

Great improvements took place during this year of 1774, when a new bridge was built over Stoupe Beck - the labourers were well plied with beer, at a cost of 1s. 8d. for 'all the workers'. Obviously a good structure, it lasted until 1820, with maintenance costs of £1. 9s. 3d. The new bridge, in 1820, cost all of £4. 18s. 1d. They also had to keep the roads clear - one entry records the payment of 'one shilling (5p) for taking a dead horse from Lingers

14,15,16. (above l.) 'Bay Bank, the main approach to the village and some of its quaint side streets (above r.) Kings Beck from Chapel Street, and (below) the aptly named Bloomswell.

17,18,19. *The village's public houses were involved in the smuggling trade. (above l.) The Mariners in The Square reputedly had a tunnel to the clifftop. (r.) The Fisherman's Arms, scene of the incident of the brandy kegs. (below) The Dock built over subterranean tunnel.*

Hill to the sea cliff'. (Any extra for pushing it over?) A good time was had by all at the annual choosing of the surveyors, when they spent all of two shillings (10p) on beer!

Many of the roads were still just rough tracks - 'turf roads' from the moors which were used for carrying peats down for fuel for fires - and these were used frequently by the smuggling fraternity, so it was in their interest to give their 'statute days' with a little more willingness than may have been usual. A reasonably well maintained road could mean the difference between safe disposal and capture if the smugglers cart became stuck! Sledges were used on tracks too deeply rutted for the speedy and safe passage of carts.

Occasionally they must have been too busy, or less diligent, as highway records show fines for neglect. In 1788 Fylingdales and Hawsker Parishes were fined jointly for neglect to the moor road; in 1824 the road from Thorpe Green to the Parish Church must have got a bit rough, for a fine of £30 was imposed on the two Parishes jointly. But in 1826, a massive fine of £400 was imposed by the Quarter Sessions, and that must have taken some finding!

The old route across the moors was so dangerous and difficult that travellers on horseback hired a guide at Pickering in order to reach Whitby without mishap.

The area surrounding 'Bay was, therefore, one of the toughest assignments for the 'law keepers'.... but the coin had another, well polished side, for locals who were well versed in the secrets of these treacherous tracks across the bogs could use them to distinct advantage!

In this context, we meet surely the most dramatic and colourful personality of this whole era - the beautiful Jiddy Vardy.

Jiddy's dark, exotic beauty and the mysterious circumstances surrounding her arrival in Bay Town, created a romantic charisma that caused mixed feelings of admiration and jealousy. The fair haired maidens of this cold northern land envied Jiddy's glossy long hair, black as a raven's wing, her sloe-dark eyes, sun-warmed skin, and tall athletic figure. The married women eyed her slyly with suspicious jealousy, and issued their husbands with dire threats if they became emotionally involved with this bewitching 'gipsy', and many Bay Town men must have stoically suffered their wives' displeasure as they defiantly continued to associate in the company of this extraordinary and brave young woman. The wives may have curbed their jealous anger if they had only understood the real nature of Jiddy's friendship with their menfolk! Could they but have known the true facts, many would have realised that they owed their husbands' very lives to Jiddy's courage and ingenuity.

Jiddy's sudden arrival as a young girl, in the home of an elderly, childless couple, had caused tongues to wag in an unprecedented flurry of speculative gossip. As far as could be established, her childhood had been both eventful and sad. Her dark Latin good looks were inherited from her mother, a beautiful Italian girl named Vardarelli, who had arrived in England as companion to a French noblewoman on a visit to the Court of King George II. The lovely Signorina Vardarelli had caused quite a stir in the palace of the King; plans for her secret elopement with a wealthy English Count were discovered, the Count banished from Court on some trivial mission, and Signorina Vardarelli left with an illegitimate baby daughter. The King's Court being no place for a squalling baby, the infant was promptly removed to an orphanage from where she was apparently kidnapped and held to ransom by someone who had discovered her unusual background.

20,21,22. Fisherhead (above l.) home of 'Big Isaac' McCaw. (above r.) 'The sea and the village live as one'. (below) The sun sets on an exciting chapter of history.

Plans going awry, mystery hung over the intervening years until her unexplained and unlikely arrival in Scarborough some time later. The elderly couple with whom Jiddy now lived in Bay Town would never speak of how they came to take her in as a housemaid, but one thing was certain, that it had been a favourable wind that had blown her into the lives of the people of Bay Town! ·

Jiddy's aristocratic background had bred in her an instinctive feel for the better things of life, and she quickly developed a natural skill with her needle, so was in great demand in all the big houses for dressmaking and sewing jobs. Jiddy soon learnt to listen discreetly, and thus gained much secret and useful knowledge.

She was contented living with the kind old couple, and more than happy that her earnings with needle and thread enabled her to supplement their expenses. She grew tall and fit and very athletic, and craved not for the attentions of the menfolk, though she would flirt and tease with the other village girls in their games of youthful courtship. Jiddy developed a fierce loyalty to these good people and many of those deeply involved in the smuggling activities had cause to be grateful to her keen ear, sharp eye and wise discretion.

Such a strikingly pretty girl had obvious attractions for the militia, and this, coupled with her unswerving loyalty and ability to take care of herself, gave her a distinct advantage when a little discreet flirtation could cleverly wrest vital information from the opposition!

One late November afternoon, Jiddy was visiting friends on a farm at High Normanby. As she was about to leave, some soldiers on horseback rode into the foldyard. The officer in charge asked Jiddy a number of questions, which she answered evasively, but openly enough so as not to arouse hostility. Sensing that useful information might be prised from the officer - a not unhandsome young man - Jiddy leant seductively against the door post, hand on hip, and black eyelashes fluttering alluringly. Engaging the officer in conversation, Jiddy craftily extracted the knowledge she required. Playing on the male ego, and fully aware of her magnetic physical attraction, she was quite expert in drawing the unsuspecting dragoon into revealing the fact that he was awaiting 'company'. Jiddy shifted her position against the door post, and drew her shawl tighter round her sensually attractive figure. Deliberately misunderstanding him, "Wives - or sweethearts?" she enquired in a low, sultry voice, and with a toss of her raven black hair.

The officer drew the reins tighter on his restless horse. "Oh, just friends", he replied, swinging round with a clatter of hooves, and moving off with a backward glance which left nothing to Jiddy's imagination.

She chuckled to herself; his 'friends' were surely Preventive men who may well have been on the scent of the large cargo of contraband that had been landed that very morning, and, at that precise moment in time, being prepared to start the journey inland.

As soon as the riders were out of sight, Jiddy gathered her skirts about her, and long legged and fleet of foot, ran swiftly down to the 'Bay to warn her friends that suspicion was aroused. The pack horse and sledge trains were immediately despatched, to cross White Moor to Littlebeck by daylight, where they would be safe until morning, no stranger daring to traverse that moor by night.

Shortly after dusk, word reached 'Bay that the Preventive men had joined the Dragoons, who rode into the village and down along the beach towards Stoupe Beck.

Jiddy was uneasy that if the soldiers got wind of the escape, they, with their faster, unencumbered horses, could overtake the lumbering pack animals as they toiled towards

White Moor. Quickly thinking, Jiddy made a brave plan, which, if successful, would lure the Dragoons in totally the wrong direction! Begging a ride pillion behind a young farmer - who would undoubtedly enjoy Jiddy's close company for a while - she dismounted at the top of the hill, lit her lantern and held it high where it could be seen down in 'Bay, hoping the soldiers would see it and set off to follow the 'smugglers'. Walking backwards and forwards, exposing the lantern at frequent intervals to give the impression of a number of individual lights, and arranging with the farmer to show a light in his window if the Dragoons passed his house, Jiddy made for her next point - Blea Howe. To reach this, a wide detour round the swamp at the head of Jugger Howe Beck was necessary. All the effort was worth while, when the flicker of light shone out from the farmhouse. Out came Jiddy's lantern, swung boldly for a short while as if lighting the way, then extinguished. The plan was working beautifully, and Jiddy began the long walk home. Gaining safe ground, she heard the shouts and shrieks of the Dragoons as they floundered in the bog!

Not wishing the handsome officers to suffer a slow, horrible death in the swamp, Jiddy approached cautiously, and shouted, enquiring who was in distress, and where - as if she didn't know!

Their Captain mistook Jiddy's voice for that of a farm boy, and offered her a shilling reward in exchange for fetching assistance. Returning to the 'Bay she told her story and organised help. The Preventive men were suspicious at first, on hearing the tale of their comrades in the bog, but local Bay men offered to accompany them to assist, in the hope of some amusement. They need not have feared too much for the men's safety, for by pulling and spreading heather over the bog, five of the seven 'flounderers' had already regained firm ground. The diversion, which caused some discomfort to the 'Snivs' had been successful, for the smuggler train meanwhile got clean away.

Close packed cottages crammed into secretive huddles in narrow alleyways made Baytown the ideal spot for smuggling.

Jiddy wasn't the only woman to have a laugh at the expense of the Preventives.

A common method of transporting small quantities of spirits was in pigs' bladders concealed under the skirts - somewhat delicate if handled carelessly, but profitable if these could be disposed of during normal market day transactions. An old newspaper relates the story of some ten Robin Hood's Bay women who were on their way to Whitby to market farm produce and a few carefully hidden 'extras', when they were unfortunate enough to meet Isaiah Moorsom, one of the High Officers of His Majesty's Customs. Isaiah politely stood aside on the narrow path, unsuspectingly, to let the innocent-looking women pass. Unfortunately, the last in the line couldn't keep a straight face, and her expression betrayed the fact that she was not as innocent as she looked. She was a tall, powerful woman, with a fair share of common sense. Keeping Isaiah at arms length, she turned and began to walk back towards Robin Hood's Bay, Isaiah following, whilst her nine companions headed safely on towards Whitby.

Isaiah was pondering the best way of tackling this Amazonian female, being somewhat of a dandy, and immaculately turned out in knee-breeches, white silk stockings, and polished black leather silver-buckled shoes - hardly the gear for scrambling in the mud! Taking advantage of his sartorial elegance, the clear-headed, quick-witted lady, on reaching a stile, leapt nimbly over, and gathering her skirts, dashed off down the muddiest track she could find. Reluctantly following, poor Isaiah soon became bogged down, and found his immaculate white stockings spattered with mud to the knee. The long-legged nimble female was soon out of reach, and Isaiah gave up the chase, but the indignity remained in his mind for many weeks, and he was heard to remark to the lady's husband some time later, "Robert, your wife did play me a bonny trick!"

A visitor to a nearby coastal village, entering up his diary in 1799, wrote - 'In going down the hill we met several females whose appearance was so grotesque and extraordinary, that I could not imagine in what manner they had contrived to alter their natural shape so completely; till upon enquiry, we found that they were smugglers of spiritous liquors which they were at the time conveying by means of bladders fastened under their petticoats, and, indeed, they were so heavily laden that it was with great apparent difficulty they waddled along.'

Even the famous Victorian novelist Elizabeth Gaskell, on visiting Whitby during her researches for the locally based novel 'Sylvia's Lovers', was intrigued, and probably secretly admiring of the cunning ways of the fairer sex. 'The clever way in which certain women managed to bring in prohibited goods show how, in fact, when a woman did give her mind to smuggling, she was more full of resources and tricks and impudence and energy than any man.'

Some women passengers on ships made the most of the 'duty free' - one titled lady was caught in possession of one hundred and fourteen Parisian silk dresses - an excessive wardrobe on a sea voyage - even for a Duchess! In fact, the female opportunists became so blatantly cheeky that in some main ports an official woman 'searcher' had to be appointed. In smaller places, such as Whitby, searches, when necessary, were carried out by the wives of the local Customs officers.

The role of the women, therefore, was not an insignificant one. Not only could they unobtrusively secrete small amounts of contraband within their clothing, and sell it on the 'black market', but they were extremely useful as message carriers when the dangers of the Press Gang threatened. The women could go about their daily business with a degree of smiling-faced innocence whilst their menfolk were holed up safely behind closed doors.

The odd mishap did occur, though. One morning, a Robin Hood's Bay mother and daughter were trudging along the path to Whitby after a night of heavy rain, transporting bladders of spirits concealed under their warm skirts and cloaks. The daughter, full of the joys of youth, skipped along somewhat less carefully than her staid old mother, slipped on the sticky mud, and fell - with disastrous results! As the pungent liquid oozed expensively down her legs, she exclaimed, "Ooh, moother, mi blether's brussen!"

Many such stories abound - and obviously the extent of wit and cunning was honed to the fine sharpness of sprung steel - a sophisticated game of 'cat and mouse' on both sides.

Robin Hood's Bay was the most favoured landing place on the coast, although the immediate hinterland afforded more difficult terrain than that at Sandsend or Upgang, where the shore was flatter and sandier, and where the numerous tracks across the Cleveland Hills gave quicker and easier access. However, the 'Bay had the advantage of being the safest place; its cliff edge cottages having windows and signalling points which could be visible to smuggling ships right across the Bay - but signalling was a risky business, with severe fines of up to £500 or six month jail sentences for being careless enough to get caught. Being the headquarters of the smuggling activities on this part of the coast, the wily Yorkshire wit devised many elaborate and cunning warning systems, though not all were by any means perfect, and smugglers had many narrow escapes.

However, Dame Fortune is a fickle female, and things occasionally went wrong, with quantities of goods seized, but only rarely were the smugglers themselves actually caught or seen clearly enough for identification. Anonymity was preserved at all costs. Injuries were not uncommon, considering the frequent violence which erupted between smuggler and Preventive.

After one particular encounter, a smuggler was severely wounded in the leg, and assisted off the shore, into the comparative safety of a farm house near Bay Mill. A Doctor Mewburn was called in and discovered the injuries to be so severe that amputation was necessary. News leaked out, and later Dr. Mewburn called upon to give evidence, but was unable to identify his patient, whose face had been covered with a cloth throughout the operation - no doubt in danger of suffocation in addition to his other worries! But being of tough Yorkshire constitution, he recovered and was smuggled out of the area. Some time later, a one-legged seaman was employed on the quay at Lowestoft. He wore a Robin Hood's Bay pattern gansey!

Each port along the coast had its own traditional pattern by which a seaman could be identified. Most of the stitches represented aspects of fishing, such as ropes, nets both empty and full of fish, fishbones, ladders, marker flags, and rocky or sandy beaches. The traditional Robin Hood's Bay pattern is a fairly plain one, with stripes of 'rope' and 'sand'. The garments were closely knitted from 5 ply oiled wool, on sets of five or seven needles so as to be seamless - and were windproof and weatherproof. A Sunday best version or 'Bridal Shirt' was knitted by a young fisherman's new bride as a betrothal gift - worn at his wedding and other special occasions, and finally as his burial shroud.

'A one-legged seaman was employed on the quay at Lowestoft. He wore a 'Bay pattern gansey!'

Unwelcome visits by Customs and Excise and Press Gangs certainly held up business whilst they were in the vicinity, but possibly the greatest danger was of traitors in the camp. In 1736, the threats and attacks on Revenue officers had increased to such an extent that the Government introduced the first of the Smuggling Acts, in which the death penalty was introduced for wounding an Officer of the Crown, unarmed smugglers faced flogging or deportation, and any who betrayed the names of his associates was granted a free pardon. Thus all strangers were viewed with suspicion. 'Better the devil you know, than the devil you don't' was an apt proverb of those times, and gave rise to an attitude which remained in Bayfolks' blood even to within living memory, and strangers were stoned out of the village.

However, these new laws made the smugglers even more determined not to get caught, and they became well organised gangs which did not stop at intimidation, torture and murder.

A cottage somewhere on Fisherhead was known to be the headquarters of the Bay smugglers - the home of one 'Big Isaac' McCaw, who together with his friends and accomplices Silas Biddick and Sandy Kellock, planned a dangerous exploit one dark October night.

During the day, an unpopular resident nicknamed 'Gobbit', by reason of his big mouth, had been spotted sneaking off in the direction of the Customs headquarters at Scarborough. False rumours had been rife the previous few days, regarding a 'landing' at Ravenscar, and Gobbit's big ears had caught wind of the odd snippet of deliberate gossip - enough to send him scurrying off on his tale-bearing mission. Gobbit was not a 'local', had never been accepted in the community and was, quite rightly, suspected of being a spy. It was high time he was taught a lesson, for he was becoming uncomfortably dangerous.

Jiddy Vardy entered the smoky room of the cottage with a broad smile. She had met Zachariah Storm following Gobbit at a discreet distance to make sure he was well on his way unhindered. The Bay men, with uncanny intuition, correctly anticipated that Gobbit's tale would send forth the Revenue sloop from Scarborough. Zack Storm took up a vantage point near Burniston, and as soon as the sloop broke cover from Scarborough harbour, remounted his horse and rode back with the news that the plan was working perfectly! Isaac, Silas and Sandy put the next elaborate move into action; a team of Bay men were sent along the cliffs to Ravenscar with decoy lanterns, two local cobles 'oared up' ready to row out to meet the sloop, and the rest of the Bay awaited the arrival of the real smuggling vessel off North Cheek, to run the contraband ashore undisturbed.

Meanwhile, the lured Revenue cutter reached Ravenscar, spotted the decoy lanterns, and sailed dangerously close inshore. Ready and waiting, the coble crews with muffled rowlocks came silently alongside and boarded the sloop, Big Isaac overpowering the crew of two men and a boy single handed. Transferring the unconscious Revenue officers into a coble and setting it adrift, Isaac, Silas and Sandy hoisted sail and set off for Holland, where the sloop was sold for a large sum of money. Smugglers had turned pirate, had come home with enough money for Sandy to put his share into the purchase of a new boat, to replace one recently lost in the cause of smuggling; Gobbit left the area for good, and hearty laughs echoed over the pints of ale in the pubs for many a night to come!

Gobbit was not the first to have been obliged to leave the village 'voluntarily'. A father and two daughters by the name of Ashner lived near the Bank top, and being newcomers of only five years standing were regarded with the usual degree of suspicion. Ashner was a farm hand, Nell in domestic service, and Ann acted as housekeeper for her father.

Ashner was a good worker, but dour, and kept himself to himself. Nell was a bit of a flirt, and caused a lot of bother between a Bay girl, Betsie Arno, and the young sailor, Abe Storm, who was courting her. Abe was truly fond of Betsie, but, his male ego flattered by the attentions of the not unattractive Nell, found himself talking a bit too freely in answer to her questions about his occupation and movements. Abe became a bit suspicious, and curbed his tongue - but too late!

Down in the Dock, a flurry of activity heralded the arrival of a smuggling vessel with the message that there was plenty of 'stuff' on board if the boats would go out for it. A considerable amount of contraband was purchased for cash, and hidden in the boats under the fishing gear.

The too-prompt arrival of the Preventives on the scene caused some concern and confusion. How did they know so quickly, and how were the goods now to be safely disposed of? If discovered, not only would the goods be forfeit, but the boats confiscated as well!

The only way was to arrange a decoy; and prove at the same time that Ashner was the informer. It was not difficult to get the rumour whispered to Nell that there was to be a landing at Ravenscar that night. As expected, Nell absented herself from her job and went running home to Daddy. Ashner was observed furtively sneaking to the Customs lookout to spill the beans.

The decoy party with the lanterns drifted away in ones and twos, as a mass exodus would have aroused further suspicion. As darkness fell, they displayed their lights in the prearranged positions, and having ensured that the Preventives had seen and were on the way, left a couple of lights hanging on a whin bush, and set off back home by the cliff path, chuckling as they passed the Preventives trudging southwards along the beach far below!

Back in the Dock, the scene was one of frantic activity, as the speedy removal of goods from the boats got under way, men, women and children all lending a helping hand. Very quickly all was back to normal, apart from a few flushed faces and heavy breathing as families resumed life around their firesides. The contraband had vanished into the countless hiding places in their cottages.

News that the Preventives had all rushed off to Ravenscar spread like wildfire through the village gossips, with rumours that Nell Ashner and her unpopular father had a lot to do with the whole affair.

Betsie Arno confronted Nell with the accusation that she had only seduced Abe Storm with the intention of having him arrested and claiming informers money. Nell tearfully protested that she knew nothing about it - but rightly or wrongly, no one was inclined to give her the benefit of the doubt.

After an uproar such as that, no 'foreigner' could possibly stay in the Bay, so Ashner and his daughters moved to Whitby, and Betsie Arno made certain that she got Abe Storm to the altar before he succumbed to the flattering charms of any other young ladies.

There are two sides to every story, and to perhaps save face in an ignominious situation, the Customs officers could well be forgiven for making out a report in their favour.

Soon after three men in the Preventive Service - Henry Downsham, John Wellow and David Evans - had been stationed at Robin Hood's Bay, they were involved in a very nasty incident. Their official report reads: 'Were returning to Quarters on duty from Whitby. Were set upon quickly by company of Whitby smugglers at Hawkscar. Were beaten and bound. Escaped and reached Quarters three o'clock. Did not know men in darkness.'

Rumour spread like wildfire, and this dastardly and evidently highly organised attack on the officers caused great indignation and concern all along the coast. The officers had certainly been injured and badly treated, and even though they did not normally attract sympathy, there was no doubt that public opinion was aroused in their favour. There was also deep concern that the incident would draw the attention of the authorities even closer to the Robin Hood's Bay area, and may result in the deployment of even greater surveillance with subsequent curtailment of activities. According to rumour, a murderous gang of about twenty smugglers from Whitby had waylaid the three officers, beaten them unconscious, tied them up, bundled them into a lonely shed, and left them. One, having eventually regained consciousness, struggled free and released his companions, then staggered the three miles to Robin Hood's Bay, carrying the third man who was unable to walk.

The countryside was scoured to find the villains, and the story got exaggerated out of all proportion, particularly upsetting the residents of Bay Town because of the official report which could have severe repercussions and invite a clampdown on all operations in the area.

Naturally, the officers claimed they had put up a strong fight, and had retaliated with vigour before being outnumbered, overpowered, and brutally beaten unconscious. Of course, no one in Whitby confessed to the crime, neither was anyone 'shopped' - and the affair faded into one of the seven day wonders for which the Bay is still famous!

When you consider the other side of the story, it is no wonder no one from Whitby got 'shopped' - because there was no one! The two men who were concerned kept silence until they were quite elderly and safe from recriminations. The odd secretive smile and knowing wink of the eye must have passed between the two of them from time to time, but their hold on their tongues was admirable, because it was the kind of tale to earn countless rounds of free drinks in the pub!

The two silent men of the story were James Linskill who lived with his sister Alys in a little cottage near Stainsacre, and Jonas Chaplow from Hawsker. At the time of the controversy they were both about thirty years old, powerfully built men, ostensibly farm workers, but had fingers in more than one smugglers 'pie'.

On the night in question, they had been involved in a landing at Hawsker Bottoms, a steep-cliffed coastal indentation between Robin Hood's Bay and Whitby, a lonely spot with the only access to the shore being the treacherous zigzag path known as the Donkey Road - a fairly safe landing place, even in broad daylight, but lethally dangerous in the dark. James and Jonas had taken the responsibility of hauling the goods up the cliff and arranging despatch. 'Borrowing' a sledge from the farm where they worked - probably Spring Farm - they sent off their load as soon as darkness fell. The driver was instructed to leave two barrels hidden under a pile of bracken in an old shed which was used as a sheep shelter about a mile from the coast at Knipe Howe cross roads. James and Jonas had planned to collect their tubs as soon as the other sledges and pannier horses were safely on their way.

As the two men set off inland, with the job well done, it began to rain heavily, and as the sheep shelter came into view, they decided to go in and keep dry for a while. Checking that their own two tubs of spirit had been hidden under the bracken as instructed, they leant against the doorway and lit up a couple of companionable pipes of tobacco - secreted on the same run - to while away the time whilst the rain eased off. In the faint light from the watery moon, three silhouetted figures became visible, approaching the sheep shelter. Too late to make a run for it unobserved, the safest plan of action was to hide. Some branches had been wedged across the rafters to form a makeshift hayloft, to which a rickety ladder gave them access to a somewhat precarious perch.

Preventive men did not like getting wet any more than anyone else, and so they also decided to take refuge in the sheep shelter! Floorspace was somewhat limited, therefore it was only a matter of time before one of them stubbed his toe on one of the concealed barrels! The sound of heavy leather boot knocking against wooden spirit tub was not an unfamiliar sound to the sheltering Preventives. To their astute minds, it was apparent that the tubs had not been there for very long, and not likely to remain there much longer, either.

The smugglers could return at almost any moment. For sure, the Preventives needed help, but how to safely send for it posed quite a dilemma. The smugglers might already be on their way, and one man running into them on his own would not receive a very gentle welcome. To send out two and leave the third alone in the sheep hut could be just as dangerous. Finally, they agreed to stick together and wait, as a search revealed only the two tubs - a load requiring only one man to collect. Just to make sure that there was no further hidden contraband, one of the officers decided to fill in time by having a look in the hayloft! Grasping hold of one of the supporting branches, he began to heave himself up, but he was a big, heavy man, and the branch only intended for supporting hay was already overweighted with the hefty bulks of James and Jonas! Not surprisingly, it broke, depositing the heavy officer awkwardly and painfully on the ground, hurting his back and hip quite badly.

James and Jonas edged warily back against the wall, towards a glimmer of light which showed through a displaced stone in the gable end. With a bit of luck, the noise of the rain would disguise their effort to loosen the rough thatch and gain them an escape route. James pushed a little too enthusiastically, dislodging a loose stone which clattered noisily to the ground outside the building.

"Sh! Listen! He's out there!" whispered the officers. "You go that way round, and I'll go this, and we'll surprise him!" The surprise was turned on them, however, as, armed with heavy sticks, they cautiously crept in the pitch darkness, one either side of the building, and encountered - not a dastardly smuggler - but each other!

Laying on heavy blows, one finally, unknowingly knocked out his mate, the unfortunate Henry Downsham. Meanwhile, back in the safety of the sheep shelter, James and Jonas hid in the shadows, falling on the returning 'sniv', overpowering him and binding him hand and foot. The battered Henry Downsham, retrieved from behind the shed, was likewise secured; the injured man groaning and writhing on the floor posed no threat - it would have taken him a long time to run for help with his broken leg and painful back.

James, very courteously under the circumstances, apologised for having to leave the men gagged, bound and disarmed, but, he explained reasonably, they would otherwise be off to Whitby to raise the alarm. As he was going that way himself, he lied, he would send assistance in his own good time. Hence the rumour that a Whitby gang was involved in the attack, and no one, until years later, was ever any the wiser - only James and Jonas as they departed to their homes in Hawsker and Stainsacre ever knew the truth of that escapade.

Whilst they were thus occupying the 'snivs', who knows what might have been going on in Robin Hood's Bay? Whilst the cats were away, the Bay mice could have been having a field day!

Hawsker Bottoms, where James and Jonas landed goods.

That was not the only confrontation which was reported between the deadly duo and the three wise men from Bay!

Our unpleasant sea frets or 'haars' do have their advantages, especially to astute locals like James and Jonas who knew every nook and cranny of the landscape even in pitch darkness. One foggy morning, the two of them were tidying up the loose ends of another run into Hawsker Bottoms, which had been landed in the early hours of the morning, and hauled up via Maw Wyke Stye. A good haul of six and a half ankers of gin (about 26 gallons) plus a quantity of small one and a half gallon tubs had to be delivered to Whitby. Under cover of the fog, even though it was broad daylight, the two J's decided to move the goods away from the cliff and hide them in Hawsker before proceeding to Whitby at a more favourable time. There was just too much for two sledge loads, so a third was necessary for the 'dregs'. The first two had safely gone on their way, and James was following up with the third, when he heard voices coming through the fog. Hurrying the pony over some rough ground across the main highway, the sledge bounced and a tub fell off, unbeknown to James in his hurry. As he feared, the voices belonged to his three companions of the sheep shelter! The wispy fog cleared sufficiently to treacherously expose the tub sitting eloquently in the middle of the road, right in front of their eyes!

Coming up the road some distance behind, Jonas, who had been making all tidy at the cliff edge before following on, saw the gin tub sitting there and the three men raising their tricorne hats and scratching puzzled heads.

Whistling a tune, hands casually in pockets, Jonas sauntered up and was about to wander past when he was stopped and interrogated. The ability to keep a quick witted tongue, a clear cool head, and a steady beating heart became a necessary requirement in dealing with unexpected situations, and the courage to face out such encounters with a degree of good humour was one of Jonas's strong points. A bantering conversation ensued in which Jonas, naturally, denied any knowledge of the lonely gin tub, sitting there all by itself in the middle of the road.

Casually sauntering round it and cheekily poking at it with his foot, he cleverly turned the conversation to imply that it had been brought by the 'snivs' themselves from Whitby, and that they were having a well-earned rest.

Drawing away from the group, he casually sauntered on his way, until he was out of sight, whereupon he took to his heels and ran to find James.

James, by now, had returned to Spring Farm, where his companions had stowed the bulk of the run in the cellar of the house, unbeknown to the occupants. He had discovered a small door, well concealed behind a corn bin in a stable adjoining the house, and of course, James's presence in that vicinity aroused no suspicion whatever. To make absolutely sure, it was quite usual to stall a 'kicker' - a bad-tempered horse - in that particular stable, and no one but James and Jonas could handle the animal.

It was not so much the loss of the gallon and a half of gin which bothered them - plenty more where that came from - but the fact that the 'Snivs' now had solid evidence that running was taking place in the Hawsker area; this had hitherto been a fairly safe district for landing, with access into Whitby by way of the secluded and heavily wooded Glen Esk.

The goods which James and Jonas and company were dealing with, very likely had been landed from one of the most notorious smuggling vessels plying this coast with a regular supply of goods from the Dutch port of Flushing (now called Vlissingen). For many years during the 1770s, the schooner 'Kent' was one of the most serious thorns in the side of the Preventive Service. She was a good sized vessel, with a 77 foot mainmast, heavily armed with sixteen four-pounder carriage mounted cannon, twenty swivel guns, and blunderbusses and muskets for her forty-strong crew.

Much of the 'Kent's' activities were carried on at night, where her black tarred hull was almost impossible to discern in the darkness. She had several close encounters with the locally based revenue cutter, 'Swallow', under the command of Captain Mitchell.

Poor Captain Mitchell had a rough time chasing around the Bay after smuggling vessels. Although he had a crew of fourteen men, which indicates a ship of some reasonable size, he generally came off worst. His other main problem was David 'Smoker' Browning, a smuggler who operated a cutter of some 130 tons, a forty-strong crew, fourteen carriage-mounted guns, four three-pounder cannon, and a deadly collection of swivel guns. On April 24, 1777, Mitchell attempted to drive 'Smoker' from Robin Hood's Bay, but was warned off in no polite terms. In May of the same year he had two further unsuccessful encounters with 'Kent', and in September was ignominiously fired on and damaged by another large 'free trader' off Runswick Bay. He obviously did his best to patrol the coast, but was clearly frustrated by his inferiority.

Until the July of 1777, the 'Kent' had outgunned the smaller vessels and continued to trade with impunity. However, all good things come to an end, and the 'Kent's' days were numbered.

Her ruthless Captain, George 'Stoney' Fagg, had been audaciously trading up and down the coast as usual, when word was despatched up to two large excise vessels, stationed in the Firth of Forth, that Captain Mitchell and 'Swallow' had cornered Stoney Fagg and his notorious smuggling schooner 'Kent', and with assistance, could rid the coast of this sea-faring pest once and for all. The strong northerly wind brought the excise cruisers 'Royal George', under the command of Captain John Ogilvie, and 'Prince of Wales', captained by Lewis Gillie, onto the scene at great speed, and Stoney Fagg must have had the instinctive feeling that this was the end. Captain Ogilvie sailed the 'Royal George' within earshot, and shouted to Stoney to surrender, or he would fire into her. Arrogant and brazen to the end, Stoney shouted back - 'Fire away, and be damned to you'.

Captains Ogilvie and Gillie had planned their tactics carefully, and manoeuvred 'Royal George' to port and 'Prince of Wales' to starboard of the 'Kent'. Stoney was truly the 'meat' in the sandwich, and although he put up a brave fight, shooting away the 'Prince of Wales's' bowsprit, the opposition was too great, and his final demise came with the arrival of the Royal Naval frigate 'Pelican' which sailed in and completed the capture. The shattered 'Kent' and her unladen cargo of 7,728 gallons of geneva, 3,540 lbs of tea, and 107 lbs of coffee, was towed away to the Customs House in Hull, to the moral and financial satisfaction of the Revenue Department (there was duty to the value of almost £5,500 on that cargo alone) and the rueful despair of the smuggling fraternity. There was value in that remaining 'stuff'; money's worth that could have seen many a smuggler's family comfortably through the coming winter.

The 'Kent' - notorious smuggling schooner,
captained by the swashbuckling George 'Stoney' Fagg

For many years during the 1770's the 'Kent' was one of the serious thorns
in the side of the Preventive Service. She was a good sized vessel with a
77 foot high main mast, heavily armed with sixteen four-pounder
carriage-mounted cannon, twenty swivel guns, and blunderbusses and muskets for
her forty-strong crew.

The integrity of the Customs officers was sometimes called into question; it was suggested that frequently they were in the position to have a nice little black market business going themselves. By retaining just enough captured goods to provide sufficient evidence, the rest found its way into profitable outlets, or convenient bribes. Official letters have been unearthed which clearly show that this most certainly went on in Whitby, and that the Collector of Duty, a Mr Hamlet Woods, between 1722 and 1724 is recorded in these letters as having sent over a hundred gallons of ale and four lots of fish to Edward Williams, of the Board of Examiners in London, also gifts of 'countrey ale' and dried fish to Abram Rickards of the Inspectors Office, ale again to a Mr Dawson of the Seizures Office, and to a Mr Savage of the London Customs House a gift of an eleven gallon cask of 'Countrey Ale'. Most of these acceptable little presents had been shipped from Whitby by a Captain William Lyth on his ship 'Mary' - ironically, he had to recruit a new carrier in 1724 as Captain Lyth and 'Mary' were arrested - for carrying contraband!

Officially, goods seized by the Customs were sold, but it was evidently quite easy for the officials to retain enough for their own profitable little sidelines.

The peak of the smuggling period was the greater part of the 18th century when potentially high profits made it into big business for those willing to take the risks. Generally, circumstances favoured the smugglers; with their intimately familiar knowledge of the peculiarities of their immediate coast and country, they were at a considerable natural advantage over the Revenue men, whose thankless task was carried out in completely strange and dangerous terrain. Remember that the local surroundings then were very different from what they are today.

It was, of course, quite impossible for the Customs and Excise department to recruit 'local' personnel!

But for those who did gain employment from harrassing their fellow man, an 'honest' if modest wage was generously supplemented by 'perks', prize money, and a percentage of the sale of captured goods, just as many jobs today are made attractive by various sales incentives. The Preventives kept a weather eye open for likely informers, and rewarded reliable 'grasses' well, though it must have been very difficult to have been an 'informer' in a close knit community like that of 'Bay, where everybody still has an uncanny instinct for knowing everyone else's business! The Ashner family were cases in point - turning the old proverb inside out - 'if you can't join 'em, BEAT em'!

The 'war' at sea between 'free traders' and revenue is, as one would expect on this ideally rugged coastline, a long and complex story on its own. But, as on land, the battle was an uneven one, with the law-breakers far outnumbering the law-keepers.

In May 1777, the Collector at Hull wrote to the Board in London, complaining that a large lugger, extensively armed, was frequently to be seen in the Whitby area. He described 'Smoker' Browning's vessel, the 'Porcupine' - (well named for such a prickly customer) - as 'greatly an over match' for any of the Revenue cutters, or even for a joint attack by two of them, and that whilst he was allowed to so blatantly 'insult' the coast, there was little prospect of success in drawing him off.

Another frustrated revenue Captain, as we have already heard, was Captain Mitchell of the 'Swallow'; another the master of the revenue cutter 'Mermaid' who had several brushes with the enemy, being chased off and fired upon until realising that as well as being vastly outnumbered, they were undermanned and underequipped, retreated, ignominiously licking their wounds.

Many of the Revenue boats were rowing and sailing cobles, with crews who were no match for the local fishermen with their superior seamanship and knowledge of local conditions. On many occasions the Revenue men felt it more prudent to turn a blind eye rather than force an arrest which would arouse keen local feelings.

Customs and Excise Officers on local duties were frequently disorganised, poorly paid, and often fought over the prize money which was not always paid by the Government. They depended greatly on informers, whom they rewarded generously.

However, it paid to be diligent, even under trying circumstances; the incentive to seize goods encouraging, for prize money could well exceed an officer's regular and moderate pay by large amounts. Half the total prize money from seizures went to the Government, the remaining half being shared proportionately

The Revenue Cutter "Swallow", commanded by Captain Mitchell,
with a crew of fourteen men was no match for 'Stoney' Fagg,
and David 'Smoker' Browning with his 'Porcupine'.
As well as being vastly outnumbered, the Revenue Cutters
were comparatively undermanned and underequipped.

among the crew - half to the Captain, a quarter to the Mate, and the remaining quarter among the crew. A good haul made by the 'Mermaid' on one of her luckier days, amounted to 336 gallons of brandy, 1,519 gallons of gin, 2,100 lbs of tobacco, and 60 lbs of tea - a total excise duty value of £2,318 on the spirits alone! The crew of that particular captured vessel all claimed to be Belgians, to avoid being charged by the British authorities and either jailed or sent into the navy!

But all good things come to an end, and by the mid 1800's, smuggling was gradually decreasing. In 1822 the Coast Guard was founded by order of the Prince Regent, and by the end of the decade was operating fully and efficiently. It fulfilled a dual purpose, by supplementing the hard-pressed Customs and Revenue with stations at strategic coastal points, manned by tough ex-seamen who were thus given useful employment after the end of the Napoleonic wars.

Gradually taxes were reduced on dutiable goods; it had evidently dawned on the Chancellor of the Exchequer of the time that vastly more revenue was being lost through smuggling, and that the Government would, in fact, make more money by reducing taxes on dutiable goods to an extent whereby the risks involved by the smugglers now far outweighed the monetary rewards! It had taken the politicians about a hundred years to work out the logistics of that theory!

Sadly, the inhabitants of old Robin Hood's Bay didn't look at it that way. One ancient worthy was heard to say; 'Alas, there's no smuggling now and poor folks ha'n't got the means o' bettering themselves like proper Christians'!

Robin Hood's Bay remains today, a unique village, hidden away by the North Yorkshire moors. The cottages stand, as they stood in the past, cheek by jowl, with the fury of the North Easterly gales and storms continually being hurled against their walls. The village and the sea live as one.

Some cottages have yielded their secrets, others not; they remain silent, wrapped in the aura of their own mysterious past - and so, the end of an exciting, profitable, and entertaining chapter of our history draws to a close, but not completely, for, as in the law of physics that matter cannot be destroyed but only changed in form, smuggling still goes on today. But twentieth century smuggling has a far more sinister effect than that carried on by our tax-dodging ancestors. Drugs, armaments, explosives, and disease-carrying animals are a much more serious threat to the wellbeing of mankind than the odd illegal glass of brandy or pipe of tobacco.

It certainly is a 'rum do' and no mistake!

"Alas, there's no smuggling now and poor folks ha'n't got the means o' bettering themselves like proper Christians!"

Appendix

A description of Robin Hood's Bay from 'A Guide to Scarborough and Environs ' by Schofield - 1787;-
Younger readers should be aware of the old printers habit of using the letter 'f' in place of some 's', which makes it quite hard, but amusing to read!

ROBIN HOOD's BAY

'To the N.E. of Scarbrough, diftant 13 miles and a half. It is a fifhing town often vifited by ftrangers, attracted by the fame of its Alum Works, and the curiofity of its grotefque appearance; it is the habitation of numerous fifhermen, and their wives, with SWARMS of children.

Whether the healthinefs of the profeffion itfelf, or their ordinary diet, which is fifh, be the efficient caufe of their abundant fertility, naturalifts and philofophers, muft determine; but it is a univerfal remark, that fifhermen have proportionably, more children, than any other defcription of perfons among us. One spefies of food, they themfelves partly attribute it to, and that is, falt fifh; but moft efpecially dried Scate, which for reafons we leave others to explain, goes by the name of merry meat.

THE quantity of thefe forts of fifh which are dried at Robin Hood's Bay, as well for home confumption, as exportation is furprizing. The fronts of the houfes, are often hung therewith, and the neighbouring paddocks, covered by them, as they are fpread to dry. Poffibly the number in this part of the world is fmall of thofe whofe tafte agrees, in other points alfo, with King James I. - "If," faid he, "I was to invite the devil to take a dinner with me, I would have three difhes; firft, a Pig; fecond, a falt poll of Ling, and muftard; third a pipe of Tobacco for digeftion."

THE Scate, which is dried, without falt, only by the wind and fun, forms a part of victualling for the Eaft-India Company's fhips, it being lefs liable to corrupt and decay, than falt fifh, in hot climates; and is moreover faid to contain abundance of nourifhment, without being either hard of digeftion, or apt to breed the fcurvy. It alfo is much in ufe during the winter months, among people of various denominations, in this country. FISH and POTATOES being by many deemed (coaftwife) the ftaff of Yorkfhire life!

94

A PERSON well acquainted with the road, is indifpenfible for conducting you to this place. It is by no means a good carriage way; therefore, and from its diftance is beyond the reach of an airing on horfeback for ladies, and is ufually vifited by gentlemen only. On previous notice, fifh, often very fine Turbot, may be fupplied at the inn; but as the market is neither exquifite, nor held oftner than once a week, you have an indifferent chance, unlefs fomething be fent on, or conveyed with you. To manage, if poffible, fo as to be prefent when the fifhing boats come in, is entertaining. In good weather, it may almoft deemed a fifh fair; but the view on reaching the fummit of the mountain, above the alum works, is altogether noble. Its height is great, and the defent, which is generally preffered on foot, long and tedious.'

He then preceded recommending visiting the alum works on the cliffs between Robin Hood's Bay and Ravenscar, by describing the manner in which alum is extracted and refined - a smelly purpose, as stale urine was largely used in its production!

'THE interior alum works, are well worth feeing; and to trace the procefs will fix it laftingly in the recollection. We do not recommend the effluvia perceptible on entering the boiling houfe, for its deliciofnefs; but there being nothing in the fmalleft degree noxious, it may be guarded againft very fufficiently, by filling the noftrils with a little tobacco.

THE paffage from the works, to the village, is along the beach; which at certain times is impaffable, from the flowing in of the tide: nor is it reckoned fafe to attempt it, unlefs there be a wide fpace of fand uncovered by the water, or elfe the tide is ebbing.'

Edward H. Simpson